The Irish
Bed & Breakfast
Book

The Irish Bed & Breakfast Book

FIFTH EDITION

BY FRAN SULLIVAN
AND ELLEN SULLIVAN TAYLOR

PELICAN PUBLISHING COMPANY
GRETNA 2003

First edition, September 1994
Second printing, May 1995
Second edition, July 1996
Third edition, January 1998
Fourth edition, March 2000
Fifth edition, January 2003

*The word "Pelican" and the depiction of a pelican are trademarks
of Pelican Publishing Company, Inc., and are registered
in the U.S. Patent and Trademark Office.*

Library of Congress Cataloging-in-Publication Data

Sullivan, Fran.
  The Irish bed & breakfast book / by Fran Sullivan and Ellen Sullivan
Taylor.— 5th ed.
    p. cm.
Includes index.
  ISBN 1-58980-088-5 (alk. paper)
  1. Bed and breakfast accommodations—Ireland—Guidebooks. 2.
Ireland—Guidebooks. I. Taylor, Ellen Sullivan. II. Title.
  TX907.5.I73 S85 2003
  647.94417'03—dc21
                                          2002009519

Illustrations by Linda Lewis, Jessica Dominguez, Ellen S. Taylor, and Fran Sullivan

Front cover: *Culbidagh House (County Antrim) illustration by Fran Sullivan*

Information in this guidebook is based on authoritative data available at the time
of printing. Prices listed are subject to change without notice. Readers are asked
to take this into account when consulting this guide.

Printed in Canada

Published by Pelican Publishing Company, Inc.
1000 Burmaster Street, Gretna, Louisiana 70053

We dedicate this book to Frank,
who loved Ireland, its people, and its music so much
and because he worked so hard to make this
an exceptional book and a tribute to Ireland.

Contents

Northern Ireland

Acknowledgments

We wish to thank Rebecca Price and Mildred Schmalz for their help in preparing the new edition and handling computer/word-processing tasks. Many thanks to Ellen Taylor for her artistry; to Phillip Kidd for helping us with e-mails; and to Emily Taylor for her great typing skills.

Thank you and kudos to Carol Mooka, my sister, for driving all through Ireland on the left side as cooly as can be.

Also, we would like to thank our friends in Ireland who operate bed and breakfasts for their advice on current trends in Ireland. Much of the success of this book is due to their judgment on how the book could better serve the traveling public and be consistent with the realities of operating a bed and breakfast, or other lodging, in Ireland. In addition, we wish to thank former Town and Country Home Association president, Vera Feeney, in Spiddal, County Galway; another past chairman, Dympna Casey, Mulligar, County Westmeath; Cecilia Kiely, Blarney, County Cork; Helen Sheehan, Kilkenny Town; Carmel O'Gorman, County Cork; and especially Eileen Kelly, Clontarf, County Dublin. Eileen has generously helped us in many ways over the years. All these Irish consultants operate their own bed and breakfasts with the highest standards.

The Irish
Bed & Breakfast
Book

IRELAND

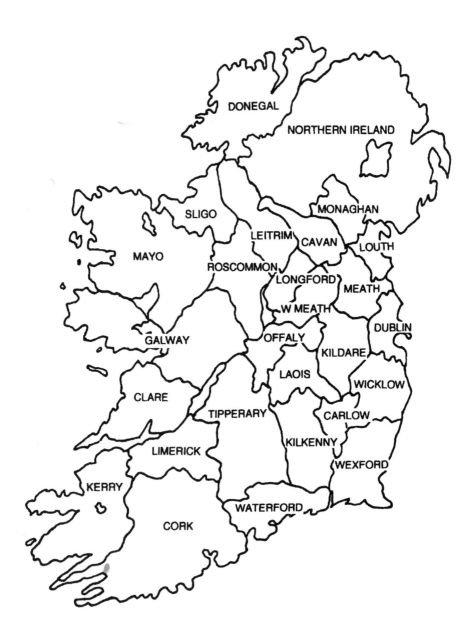

Introduction to the Republic of Ireland

BACKGROUND

Ireland is a land of outstanding beauty, serenity, and mystical charm. Its people and land have been propelled through history by dramatic and devastating events. Yet, the people possess a wonderful personality that is loving, kind, friendly beyond compare, hospitable, devout, infectiously fun-loving, witty, and always ready to tease or crack a joke.

When one decides to travel abroad in a foreign land, one must ask the question—why Ireland? How is it different from Sweden, France, England, or other countries you are considering for a visit, assuming that cost is not a factor? In other words, what's there to see and do?

Ireland is probably one of the most beautiful countries in Europe for scenery; it is one of the best for modern and traditional music, theater, and modern and early Christian art; it has an endless chain of castles and historic sites that date back to 4000-3000 B.C.; and the warm and boundless "welcoming" of its people certainly sets it apart from all other countries.

As Irish Americans who have recently come to love the land and its people, we would say that beneath the tourist veneer exists a more fascinating land and culture than we had ever imagined or proclaimed by most travel books and brochures. As we worked on this book, we both deepened our understanding of Irish history and culture, and, in our writing, endeavored to provide the reader with enough information for his or her discovery of the Ireland beneath the surface.

Since Ireland is a relatively small country, you might expect the population to be homogeneous, but this is not so. The people of Donegal and those of the south, like those found in Kerry and Cork, are quite different. The land, many have said before, fashions the character of the people. This is certainly in evidence when you meet the industrious, more serious and somber, yet sincere people of the northwest counties and compare them with the jovial, casual, softer people of the southwest.

This travel book is meant to be a guide for you to design your own itinerary. You should read up on Irish history and the various sights you want to see and then factor in the number of days or weeks you have for your trip, and with the help of a good map, like Michelin's or Bartholemew's, plan an itinerary. Some good references to help you prepare for your trip include

Rambles in Ireland, by Monie Begley, Devin-Adair Co., Old Greenwich, CT, 1985 (still a great book on Irish culture and history; fascinating writer);

Ireland, World Book Encyclopedia, Field Enterprises Ed. Corp., Chicago and London;

Ireland: A History, by Robert Kee, Abacus Edition, Sphere Books, Ltd., 1982 (excellent but hard to acquire, since it is published in England; published as a result of a special BBC series);

A History of Ireland, by Edmund Curtis, Routledge, 6th Edition, 1961 (the favorite of many historians and general readers).

Francis Bacon's advice still holds true about travel: study the country before you go, read about its culture and history while you're there, and reflect and continue your study when you return.

When planning your trip, a good rule to follow is to allow two nights at each bed and breakfast so you don't get dizzy living out of a suitcase. If you stay only one night at a B&B, it seems like you're on a merry-go-round. You come in at night and leave the next day after breakfast and you get to the point that your days are in the car and the nights in the B&B, without ever getting to know any B&B owners, seeing any local sights, or taking advantage of the many local recreational facilities and special events.

We recommend observing the **Two-Day Rule.** Sometimes you will land at a gem of a place that tickles your fancy and want to stay longer. Don't be so rigid in your plans that you miss the unexpected pleasures of a new town or region like a country fair, a market day, or special musical or dance performance. Have a plan but stay flexible. If you travel in the shoulder season, spring and fall, you won't have to worry so much about booking ahead. But if you travel in the summer, the best B&Bs, those recommended in travel guides, will fill up early.

The Irish Tourist Board, Bord Fáilte, has offices in major cities around the world. In the U.S. it is located at 345 Park Avenue New York, N.Y. 10154. Telephone: (800) 223-6470 in the U.S., (212) 418-0800, and FAX: (212) 371-9052. In London call, 071-493-3201, and in Sydney, (02) 232-7177. They offer free guides, maps, and information booklets for almost any travel requirements or interests. Some of their guides are the *Town and Country Homes Association: Guest Accommodation* for the current year, with a B&B listing of homes providing reasonable lodgings; *Farm Holidays in Ireland,* with a listing of farm B&Bs; and the *Hotels and Guesthouses—Illustrated Guide—Be Our Guest,* for the more expensive accommodations. Be forewarned that they are not rated or graded. All that the Irish Tourist Board guides give you are the number of rooms, prices, addresses, facilities available, attractions in the area, etc., but not any rating. One does not really know if they are super places or the run of the mill. Some places have the same prices, but vary enormously in charm and value.

That's where this book comes in handy. It will allow you to stay at the best ones! The places in our book were carefully selected to give you the best lodgings in an area—that is, the ones with ambience, charm, cleanliness, hospitable hosts, good facilities and accommodations, and good value for your travel dollar. They were visited by us after being recommended by other travelers, other B&B operators, and travel agents. In order to call Ireland to book ahead, you'll need to dial 011-353- then you drop the 0 from the city number and dial the rest as given to you.

Please remember that B&Bs or guesthouses change hands and owners retire, or the quality of the accommodations changes from when we visited them. Also, the prices may change. We have tried to select only those that have all the qualities above but have staying power as well. You will find descriptions of B&Bs, town and country homes, small hotels, guesthouses, and farm B&Bs. Write us at the publisher's address with your comments—good or bad. We would love to hear from you about our listings and any new ones you could recommend for the next edition.

GUARANTEE OF STANDARDS

Bord Fáilte is the official guarantor of minimum standards for most inns, guesthouses, country homes, farmhouses, and town houses. They establish the maximum allowable rate per person, whether couples or single persons. We chose to publish only nightly rates per person for couples (which in Ireland is called the rate for "sharing"). Unless it is stated to be a double rate or the price of the room, you can determine the double or couple rate by multiplying the rate we list by two. Singles pay a higher rate if they are alone. Travel vouchers you may have obtained in an Aer Lingus package or from a travel agent are good for a standard room, one with shared bath.

Most hosts will charge an additional fee of a few pounds for a private bath, accommodations that the Irish call "a room sharing with shower/toilet en suite." In this book, "private bath" means shower, sink, and toilet unless otherwise indicated. A shared bath, usually larger than the private baths, will often have a tub, shower, sink, and toilet.

Weekend and weekly rates are sometimes available at substantial savings. A weekend rate might include two nights, two breakfasts, and a Saturday-night dinner. Inquire of the host when you make your reservation as to these special arrangments, and always notify the host in advance if you have special dietary requirements for breakfast. Evening dinner is usually reserved by noon. In many locations, the dinner at the B&B is better than you can find at the local restaurant. Those hosts who have won a Galtee Breakfast Award are especially proud of their home-cooked evening meals as well.

B&Bs displaying the green shamrock sign are those that are inspected and approved by the Board Fáilte. You can be assured of minimum standards. They are contracted to maintain certain standards and rent for approved rates. All B&Bs listed have been inspected by us and the host(s) interviewed, or have been identified by other owners and/or other experienced travelers as outstanding lodgings— usually both. The B&Bs in our *Irish Bed and Breakfast Book* are held to our required high standards.

PRACTICAL MATTERS

Getting There

Flying to Shannon or Dublin airports directly means your choices are narrowed to **Aer Lingus** (1-800-223-6537) from Boston, Chicago, or New York; **Aeroflot** (1-800-867-8774) from Washington, D.C., Miami, and Chicago; or **Delta** (1-800-241-4141) from Atlanta and New York City. You can also book a charter flight contracted by private associations and organizations such as the Ancient Order of Hibernians (AOH), Irish cultural groups, and such. Check to see if a membership fee is added on to the price of the ticket. Check in the telephone directory if you are near a large city that has a large Irish-American population, and make an inquiry about their charters. Otherwise, inquire of your local travel agent. A good travel agent can advise you about the reputation of most charter companies. We traveled American Trans Air (ATA) Charter in 1995. It was cheaper, but the flight was delayed and seats were smaller.

Usually a travel agent's voucher will be good for what the Irish call a "standard" room, one having a shared bath. In some cases you will be asked for a small supplemental fee of a pound or two to cover the cost of the private bath. One package, the Irish Heritage package, includes the services of the Irish Genealogical Research Society.

Genealogical Searches

Millions of Irish were forced to leave their homeland because of the devastation of the famine and other deprivations to seek out a better life in Australia, the United States, or Argentina. You may be descended from these hearty and valiant Irish immigrants who survived these desperate days who return to Ireland in much different circumstances as tourists and travelers. If you are, it is fun and very satisfying to investigate your roots, and possibly find living relatives. In planning your trip you might wish to avail yourself of a Registered Genealogist to assist you, so that you can set aside time to check archives and records, and visit the appropriate ancestral sites. There are many. We can recommend an excellent one: Mrs. Helen Kelly. Her mailing address is Celtic Heritage, 30 Harlech Crescent, Clonskeagh, Dublin, 14, Ireland. Her e-mail address is kellyfam@iol.ie

She and Francis Dowling have produced an excellent instructional tape for the more aggressive, do-it-yourselfers. It is very informative and leads you step by step through the process of a genealogical search. We found it educational in many ways but particularly in the sense that it explained a great deal about the geopolitical structure of early Ireland. You might want to purchase this tape, playable on Canadian and U.S. Video recorders, Searching For Your Ancestors in Ireland, Shoreway Video, Int., Ltd., at the same address above.

Using the Internet

You can access the Irish Tourist Board Web site at www.ireland.travel.ie. There you will find additonal valuable information on getting there, where to stay, recreational and current cultural events. However, don't expect to find a rating system for bed and breakfasts or as much detail as is in our book. It is a good additional tool for planning.

Money and Changing Currency

Traveler's checks are the best way to carry large sums of money. You can get free traveler's checks if you belong to one of the state AAA clubs. Just remember to bring cash to their office when you purchase their American Express checks. Checks or credit cards are not usually accepted.

When you change money in Ireland, do so at a regular commercial bank, like the Bank of Ireland, and you will get the best exchange rate. Avoid the Dublin or Shannon airport branches as they are usually a little higher than downtown in the nearby city. If you change a little money at the airport to get by for a day or two then do your big exchange in the city branch, you will do better.

B&Bs that accept credit cards are indicated in this book in the full listings. Always ask the host if they accept cards, because we found that credit-card payment is becoming more popular with Irish B&Bs. About a third of town and country-home B&Bs use them. Credit-card payment in restaurants and lodgings is a convenient way to handle your money problems. The exchange rate at the date of service is usually quite favorable, and it helps you avoid carrying a lot of cash, especially in Dublin, which has a high incidence of petty theft.

Transportation

Rental Cars

Rent your car before you arrive in Ireland. It is much cheaper. Find a reliable car-rental company through your travel agent. The agent will prebook your car with a partial payment to secure the reservation.

Be sure to check with your credit-card company as to the exact insurance coverage they provide when you wave the collision damage (CDW/LDW): which kind of cars are covered and for what time period. This is extremely important. If you rent a car, read the fine print in your credit-card brochure describing the services and benefits. If your car is totaled because of this oversight, and you have waived the car company's collision damage, you will pay for a new car replacement out of your pocket. In addition, be forewarned that rental agencies overseas are not regulated by U.S. law so be sure to rent only from companies that have a reliable track record. Your travel agent can advise you which ones are reputable.

Warning: in Dublin, be careful to read fine print on parking meters, as in many districts they need streets clear for commuter traffic, and if you are still parked there after 4 P.M. you may get towed, as we did, to the tune of a $100 fine.

And another thing: in Ireland you must drive on the left side of the road.

Buses

You can take the train to the major provincial cities, and stay in city B&Bs or inns/guesthouses. However, most of the charming B&Bs are country homes and "using the buses, sometimes you can't get there from here" as they say in Maine. The country bus systems are not very handy due to their odd schedules and frequent stops. If you are lucky to find a main route, they're fine. But check bus schedules carefully. You might take a country bus ride and it might be two days later that you can catch the return. We had to hitchhike once on the Dingle Peninsula to get to where we were going because of the strange routing and schedules of buses. Fran found bus travel fun and adventurous.

When in the big cities or when tour buses are available in the country like in the Dingle or Connemara regions, leave your car in the parking garage ("car park") and take the bus. This allows you to take a rest from driving on the left side and to enjoy the ride and sights without aggravation, and your higher perch lets you see over the hedgerows and stone walls. In Dublin and Cork especially, take the bus because the one-way streets and congestion can drive you mad.

City buses are numbered and only pick up at signs marked with their number. Knowing which number bus to catch is a little bit of a hassle, but the drivers are friendly and usually helpful. But move quickly, for bus doors open and close faster that any we've traveled on in Europe.

Weather

The climate in Ireland is like New England, but with a milder winter, not much snow, and the summers are usually cooler. You can count on rain showers whenever you go. Remember this is a small island set in the Atlantic, and ocean storms blow in quickly with intermittent rainstorms. Fortunately, they move out as quickly.

We found that layering clothing is a good technique for such a variable weather pattern. Put on light clothing, and then add a light wool sweater and rainproof jacket or coat. This way you can adjust to the weather as it changes from cool mornings to very mild or warm temperatures at noon.

Booking Ahead

Booking Outside Ireland

Book ahead for the first night after arrival and the first night before departure, preferably within a short drive from the airport. We like the towns of Ennis, Bunratty, and Adare for a Shannon departure, and Malahide, Clontarf, Drumcondra, Swords, or another north Dublin suburb for a Dublin Airport departure. They are close to the airports and also have excellent restaurants nearby, lower rates, and high quality.

You will find many excellent B&Bs in this book that describe how close they are to the international airports. Book these rooms by calling from outside Ireland. In the U.S. dial 1, then 011 (the international code for both MCI and AT&T), then 353 (the country code), then the number listed in our book. Drop the zero (0) in the city/town code. You will be surprised that no advanced payment nor credit-card charge is usually required to hold a room. The Irish are very trusting in this regard, and we urge you to cancel well in advance if your travel plans change.

Booking Inside Ireland

Booking ahead within the country only requires you to call the telephone numbers listed and tell the host when you will be arriving. You may ask directions, although we have provided directions. We find that rehearsing and/or recording the directions over the phone is advisable because some are off in the country, up a maze of rural roads. Many hosts are willing to help you book ahead at no charge if you ask them. We have found this practice to be quite reliable.

General Information about Lodgings
Rooms

Rooms in private homes are often, but not always, small, though cozy with personal touches and pretty decor. Houses built expressly to run a bed and breakfast have plenty of space in the bedrooms, lounges, and dining rooms. Also, the manor homes have large rooms with high ceilings and afford a special treat not only in spaciousness but in Old World ambience. These features are pointed out in this book in the text of the listing. However, in the country homes or older homes we have sought out those whose hosts are especially warm and genuinely friendly. We feel the warmth of the welcome far outweighs the size consideration of the rooms.

Meals

After checking in, you probably will be offered tea or coffee. The Irish tea is better than the coffee because often the coffee is instant. When you arrive, remind the host of any dietary requirements you may have, and if you want dinner, assuming you arrive early in the afternoon. Better yet, if you book ahead, indicate at that time that you would like dinner. This is a good idea if you are staying in a remote area where there aren't any restaurants nearby, or you are driving a good distance and you don't want to get back in the car again after you arrive.

A *full Irish breakfast* in this book always consists of eggs cooked to order, bacon, sausage, toast or homemade brown bread with farm-fresh Irish butter or jam (you have to ask for margarine), juice, dry cereal, and tea or coffee. Extras that might be offered are fresh fruit in season, fruited yogurt, cheeses, porridge or oatmeal, scones and/or other baked goods. Special extras, which we are finding more and more, are French toast or pancakes with syrup, smoked salmon or other fish. The portions are generous. Ask when breakfast is served, and ask for a call if you don't have a travel clock. If you have to leave early to catch a plane or train, your host will usually prepare toast and coffee for you upon request. Irish hosts are very accommodating.

If you want a vegetarian or continental breakfast, let them know the night before and they will probably provide you with the fruited yogurt, toast, fresh fruit, hot or cold cereal, muesli, and tea or coffee. The healthy eating pattern recently popular in America is catching on in Ireland, too.

Booking Tours and Events

Your host will help you book plays, Irish football matches (soccer), fishing trips, horseback riding, and all the other recreational activities in the area. If you ask your host's advice, he/she sometimes will call ahead for you. If not, get the telephone number and use the B&B's box phone, which requires 20-30p to get started. In Dublin, get the *Irish Times* or one of the tabloids and you can find advertisements for the plays and musicals. The Abbey Theatre is Ireland's national repertory company, offering plays by Ireland's best. One night at a Dublin pub with music is a special treat, such as the Abbey Tavern in Howth or Slattery's on Capel Street. The show at Jury's Hotel is elaborate and very enjoyable. Your host(s) can direct you.

Telephoning in Ireland

This can be a problem for Americans who are used to easy access and fast service. Telephoning is very different in Ireland.

There are two ways you can call inside Ireland: with coins, or with a CALLCARD (or Phonecard). CALLCARDs are purchased in local shops and post offices. They are available with so many calling units for so many Irish pounds. We used 20-unit cards and found them far superior to paying with coins. You use the CALLCARD at a telephone booth marked with a yellow band and with the *Card Phone* sign. You just put your card in the slot as indicated and dial the number. The decreasing units are indicated on a digital monitor. One unit is equal to about 20p. When you call long distance, your units will decrease much more rapidly then for local calls. Don't be surprised at the number of phone booths out of order, especially in the countryside.

When you call from your B&B, inn, or guesthouse, you can make local calls for 20 or 30p. The amount for an initial call is indicated in the digital window. Many B&Bs now have coin box telephones near the front door. You dial the number, listen for the dial tone to change when the person answers, then you put in the coin. The remaining time is indicated on a digital clock, and you put more coins in, 10p or better, when time runs out.

Phone calls from hotel rooms have a 200-300 percent surcharge. Be forewarned!

Laundry

We find packing clothes for five days and taking dirty clothes to the laundry is the best way to avoid a lot of heavy luggage.

You need to take your laundry to a local Laundromat to wash and dry your clothes. Because time is of a premium, we leave our clothes and pay to have them to be washed, dried, and folded. There is only a small additional charge for this. In inns and large guesthouses, they will send them out for you and put the charge on your bill. You send out one day and usually get them back the next. We like to deliver our clothes directly as it speeds up the process and is less expensive.

Northern Ireland

Information on practical matters for Northern Ireland can be found in that section later in the book.

Having visited the Irish Republic and Northern Ireland, we found the people in both countries to be open, generous, intelligent, and interested in other people. Many have innate wisdom. Other enduring qualities are their humility and kindness. Seldom will you meet an arrogant Irishman or one who would hurt your feelings knowingly. They like to know about your life, your story, and tell you about theirs, spiced with a little humor, and they'll go way back to ancestors.

Security

In the larger cities, such as Cork, Galway, and especially Dublin, be sure to leave nothing of value that can be seen inside your car while it is parked on the street. Lock cameras, suitcases, and shopping bags in your trunk out of view. Those B&Bs that have a locked car park off the street are much preferred in Dublin. Unfortunately, in Dublin, as in other big cities where tourists congregate, there has been a high incidence of thefts. So be careful to keep wallets in your deeper front pockets, and wear no pocketbook slung over your shoulder but carry it in front with one arm over it. One option is to buy a waist purse or fanny pack that straps around your body. Travel in pairs or larger groups if possible.

County Carlow

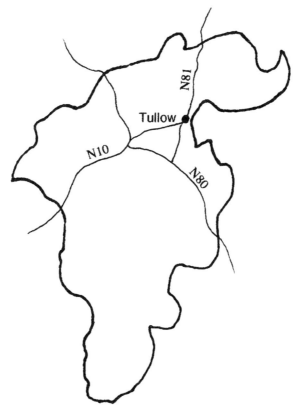

County Carlow presents you with soft rolling hills and lush pasture-land. Two important rivers run through it, the Barrow and the Slaney, which give great opportunity to avid anglers. Fish to your heart's content for pike, trout, or salmon or do "coarse" fishing. The lovely Mount Leinster is good for hiking; it is part of the Blackstairs Mountain Range along the southeast border. Near the center of the county is Ballymoon Castle. Peaceful Carlow is only an hour away from busy Dublin for a getaway vacation. It is close to Glendalough in County Wicklow, and only 10 to 15 miles away from exciting Kilkenny.

Laburnum Lodge

Anne Byrne
Bunclody Road N81
Tullow, County Carlow
Telephone: 0503-51718
E-mail: lablodge@indigo.ie
Bedrooms: 6, all with private baths
Rates: € 28-32 p.p. with bath; € 38.50 for a single; 20 percent discount for children under 12. Vouchers accepted. **Credit cards:** VISA, MasterCard. **Open:** March to November. **Children:** All ages. **Pets:** No. **Smoking:** No. **Provisions for handicapped:** Yes. 2 rooms on ground floor. Wheelchair accepted. **Directions:** There are signs posted. From the bridge in Tullow, take the N81 toward Dublin and Laburnum Lodge will be 1 mile up on the right.

This lovely new Georgian home is in the beautiful Tullow Valley surrounded by mountains. Anne is cheerful and outgoing and like a breath of fresh air. There is a feeling of bringing the outside in as there are lots of large windows, and the sliding glass doors in her dining room open onto her award-winning gardens. There is a large sun room for guests. The handsomely decorated sitting room has bold, dark-blue drapes and cream walls and the bedrooms have unusual colors such as lemon, pink, and rose. They all have orthopedic mattresses and tea/coffee facilities. Anne's Irish breakfast includes choice of eggs or French toast, and fruit, yogurt, and cheeses. We can attest to her very tasty fresh scones, which smelled baking as we entered. On a getaway weekend here you'll have access to fishing, golf (18-hole at Mount Wolseley), hunting, river cruising, signposted walks, and visits to Altamount Gardens. You may visit the historic Ring Rath or Brown's Hill Dolmen Stones or even go hang gliding nearby. Anne's brother, Jim O'Toole, wrote a book on manor houses in County Carlow.

County Cavan

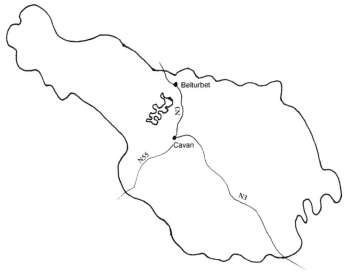

County Cavan has an odd shape, like a paramecium. The tail is sandwiched between Fermanagh and Leitrim, the head towards Monaghan, the Meaths, and Longford. It is a county of picturesque farms, lakes, and the Erne and Analee rivers. There are many good lakes for fishing, especially Lough Erne and Lough Oughter above Cavan and Butlers Bridge. This is a particularly pretty area to see. The Derragarra Inn, an award-winning pub at Butlers Bridge, has good, reasonable meals. There is a Folk Museum just across the street from it. Cavan is a bustling town with Cavan Crystal and several singing pubs. Visit Killysheen Forest Park not far from Cavan, with the ruins of Lough Oughter Castle and nature trails, swimming, and fishing. You can rent a forest chalet here by the week.

In the south of Cavan is the lovely, quiet town of Virginia amidst miles of rolling green hills, much resembling our state of Virginia. Flowers and farms abound and it borders on Lough Ramor with 22 islands in it. The lake is part of the town and adds much to its special beauty. North of Virginia is another small town known for its mention in a well-known Irish ditty. This town, Ballyjamesduff, is worth a visit. County Cavan is known for its golf and for being a crossroads.

Hilltop Farm B&B
Philomena O'Connor
Belturbet, County Cavan
Telephone: 049-9522114
Bedrooms: 10, all with private baths
Rates: €26 p.p. with bath; Single €27. 20 percent discount for children under 12. Vouchers not accepted. 4-course evening meal €20. **Credit cards:** VISA, MasterCard, Eurocard. **Open:** All year. **Children:** All ages. **Pets:** Yes. **Smoking:** Yes, 2 rooms and not in dining room. **Provisions for handicapped:** Yes, 2 rooms. **Directions:** From Cavan take the N3; farm is exactly three miles from Butlers Bridge on the right.

This fairly new house is an actual farmhouse, as Mrs. Dunne's son runs a steer and sheep farm in the back. Philomena, the gracious hostess, will greet you with tea. This bed and breakfast has clean comfortable rooms, all with pink and beige covers and cream or lilac walls. All baths are carpeted. There are sinks in every room, and the halls are stenciled. The living room has a marble fireplace, and the dining room is huge with views of the lake, which is famous for fishing. People come from all over Europe to fish here. She packs a lunch, serves fantastic evening meals, and is always ready with a cup of tea for travelers. Her Irish breakfast includes a selection of cereals, yogurt, or a bowl of fruit. You may have pancakes if you want. They serve fresh-ground coffee. There are also activities like golf, river cruising, cycling, and walking tours right in the town of Belturbet.

ALSO RECOMMENDED

Cavan Town, *Oakdene,* Ann and Paddy Gaffney, 29 Cathedral Rd. Telephone: 049-4331698. Bedrooms: 4, all *en suite.* Recommended by Brid Myles of Cavan Town.

COUNTY CLARE

County Clare

County Clare's most important feature is that it contains Shannon Airport, where everyone enters the Irish Republic who wants to see the West Coast. So that will be our starting place. If you head south toward Limerick, you'll have to see the Bunratty Castle and Folk Park. If you make reservations for the Medieval Banquet at Bunratty Castle, you'll encounter quite a wild party. If you'd like to see bright costumes, music, performers, and storytellers; try some genuine mead; and try eating a big meal with only a knife—all amidst a huge hall full of people from every country you can imagine—then you'll have a jolly, even hilarious evening. Durty Nelly's, a pub next door, is a fun place to do your first Irish singing, but it's a bit seedy.

Lough Derg and the River Shannon form the eastern edge of the county. The lengthy river finally meets the sea at the southern edge, forming a narrow bay. Killaloe, a town at the base of Lough Derg, has waterskiing, sailing, and a riverboat tour of the Lake. Also, visit the 12th-century St. Flannan's Cathedral and Ogham Stone there.

If you head northwest, you'll come to Ennis, a busy little town with a marketplace, good B&Bs, restaurants, and many singing pubs. There is a castle at Knappogue in Quin, and the Dromoland Castle is almost into Ennis. Surrounding Ennis are pretty, peaceful farmlands. From Ennis, travel north to Lahinch via the N85, which passes through Ennistymon, or go by the R476 and visit Corofin first, a good fresh water fishing spot. Here you will find the Clare Heritage Centre with lots of information for Clare genealogy seekers.

Lahinch is an interesting seaside resort with shops, quaint cafés, beaches, and lovely sea views. Horses graze on the green cliffs above the beach. To the south of here, you'll find surfing beaches at Spanish Point and the spot where ships of the Spanish Armada were wrecked. Farther south on the sea is Kilkee, with some gorgeous cliff scenery.

The most fascinating steep cliffs of fame are the Cliffs of Moher, dropping down to the sea just outside Liscannor. The cliffs are worth a look in all kinds of weather except thick fog. They are hauntingly dramatic, moss green in summer and gold-brown in fall. From the Cliffs, travel north to Doolin on the coast, where you may catch a ferry to the Aran Islands. There used to be an old custom for Aran Island boys to row over to Doolin on a specified day each year to seek a bride. Next you'll want to see The Burren, a natural geological wonder of stark, rocky hills that hold unique wildflowers, animal life, and mystical springs. You can take a walk through with a guide if you book ahead. Ask at Lisdoonvarna or Ballyvaughn. See the Aillwee Caves, too, with many stalactites and a Tea Room for a snack.

Bunratty Lodge
Mary Browne
Bunratty, County Clare
Telephone: 061-369402
Fax: 061-369363
E-mail: reservations@bunrattylodge.com
Web: www.bunrattylodge.com
Bedrooms: 5, all with private baths
Rates: €35 p.p.; 20 percent discount for children under 12. Vouchers not accepted. **Credit cards**: Yes, Visa and MasterCard. **Open:** Mid-March to November 1. **Children:** Yes, 10 and up. **Pets:** No. **Smoking:** No. **Provisions for handicapped:** None. **Directions:** Coming from Shannon Airport (on the N18), after about 4 miles take side road to Bunratty Castle, sign on left. Then take road on left between Bunratty Castle and Durty Nelly's Pub. Go 1½miles to intersection. Bunratty Lodge is two-story blue home across the intersection in country settting.

Bunratty Lodge is stunning inside and out, a stately Neo-Georgian modern home painted blue and trimmed in white, surrounded by a well-kept garden and gated entrance. The living room is spacious and elegant with a blue rug, white fireplace, and beautiful flowered drapes. The bedrooms are pink and grey or green and pink, with a myriad of flowered designs and all with thick, fluffy quilts. All the spacious bedrooms have color televisions and large tiled baths with towel heaters. Besides the full Irish breakfast, your gracious hostess, Mary Browne, serves a choice of eggs and potatoes, fruit, yogurt and cheeses, and an option of French toast. She has received the Galtee County Award for her breakfasts. The dining room is comfortable and well lighted, with large windows to the garden and choice of large table or separates. Medieval banquets at the nearby Bunratty Castle can be arranged, along with other advice on touring this area. Golf, horseback riding, swimming in the heated pool at Shannon-Shamrock Hotel, fishing, or a visit to the Folk Park behind the Castle, followed by a pint at the famous Durty Nelly's pub, are some of the local features.

Clover Hill Lodge
Anne Nash
Low Road
Bunratty, County Clare
Telephone: 061-369039
Fax: 061-360520
E-mail: cloverhill@esatclear.ie
Bedrooms: 5, all with private baths
Rates: €30-40 p.p.; 20 percent discount for children. Vouchers not accepted. **Credit Cards**: Yes. **Open:** April 1 to October 31. **Children:** Yes. **Pets:** No. **Smoking:** No. **Provisions for handicapped:** Yes, ground-floor access. **Directions:** Coming from Shannon Airport, take the N18 for 4 miles. Take the side road to Bunratty Castle, sign on the left. At Bunratty Castle, follow a sign for Low Road in front of Durty Nelly's Pub. Pass the entrance to Bunratty Folk Park, and drive up sign-posted road for about 1½ miles. House is on left.

This modern, red brick, dormered house is situated right between Bunratty Castle and Durty Nelly's, so it is easy to find. Anne will very helpful to you in finding the airport, only 10 minutes away, as well as other places of interest. Her rooms are beautifully decorated and all have orthopedic mattresses, televisions, and hair dryers. Anne gives you a choice of breakfasts from a menu. They include, juice, cereal, all Irish, fresh fruit with low-fat bio yogurt, ham slices with Irish cheese and fruit, poached or scrambled eggs, pancakes and maples syrup along with filtered coffee, herb teas, or hot chocolate. Try the medieval dinner and show at Bunratty Castle. It is lots of fun—you'll get a glass of mead, and you will be served very good period-style food while being entertained by a beautiful group of young people in period costumes. The Folk Park is worth the visit, too. Durty Nelly's is a good pub for singing and trying Guinness stout, or a good pub snack. This area gives you an early rest after your flight, and easy access to the Cliffs of Moher and coast or south to County Kerry. There is also golf, great local shopping, horse riding, and fishing nearby.

Headley Court
Kathleen Browne
Deerpark, Bunratty
County Clare
Telephone: 061-369768
E-mail: headleycourt@eircom.net
Web: www.headleycourt.net
Bedrooms: 5, all with private baths
Rates: €32 p.p.; 20 percent discount for children. Vouchers are accepted. **Credit cards:** Visa and MasterCard. **Open:** January to December. **Children:** Yes, all ages. **Pets:** No. **Smoking:** No. **Provisions for handicapped:** Yes. **Directions:** From Shannon Airport, after approximately 4 miles, take left hand turn to Bunratty. Take Low Road between Bunratty Castle and Durty Nelly's Pub. Go 1.5 miles to intersection. Turn right. Headley Court is the first house.

This attractive, modern, two-story home is painted pink with burgundy and white trim, and set among mature trees, new shrubs, and flowers. The bedrooms are bright and airy, each with its own color scheme. Some doubles have romantic canopies over them. All fabrics are coordinated, such as, navy and pink, blue and cream, or pink and white. All rooms have spacious bathrooms, tea/coffee facilities, alarm clocks, hair dryers, and color television. The furniture is eclectic with modern and antiques mixed. The living room has a maple floor with apricot colored walls and modern swag and tail curtains. The lounge is unique and handsome with its terra cotta tiles. With cheerful dining, Kathleen is an attentive host and will serve you a delicious and varied breakfast. There are the usual choices of eggs, bacon, and sausage, waffle fries, or cereal. Fruit and yogurt are also served, along with tea and coffee. Nearby, horseback riding, golf, fishing, and swimming are available. Banquet tickets can be arranged by the Brownes for Bunratty Castle.

Rockfield House
Margaret Garry
Hill Road
Bunratty, County Clare
Telephone and **Fax:** 061-364391
Bedrooms: 6, all with private baths
Rates: €40 p.p.; 20 percent discount for children under 12. Vouchers accepted. **Credit cards:** Visa and MasterCard. **Open:** January 1 to December 20. **Children:** All ages. **Pets:** No. **Smoking:** No. **Provisions for handicapped:** None. **Directions:** As you approach Bunratty Village, make a left turn after Avoca Handweavers just before Fitzpatrick's Bunratty Shamrock Hotel. You will find Rockfield House about 300 yards up that windy road on the right-hand side. There are two white eagles on the entrance gates. *Note:* Avoca Handweavers has since closed.

Beside being in the midst of all the Bunratty sights and activities, this is a very pleasant and modern home hosted by a very friendly and warm Mrs. Garry. One bedroom has a balcony and view of River Shannon. All bedrooms are pink and green and have televisions, tea/cakes, hair dryers, and electric blankets. Trouser press is in the hallway. Being perched on a peaceful hillside with the modern decor, it reminds one of California and commands a panoramic view of the River Shannon. However, the Irish wit and charm, bright and cheery rooms, and the tasty breakfast will let you know you are enjoying the best of the Irish Republic. Great brewed coffee is served along with your tasty cooked breakfast. You may choose a delicious continental or vegetarian one. All are served in a beautiful dining room that has a light green theme with lace tablecloths. A lounge with television can be enjoyed with coffeee or tea upon request. Fishing at Six-Mile Bridge, golf, swimming at the nearby hotel, or visits to nearby Bunratty Castle and Folk Park and Durty Nelly's can be arranged by Mrs. Garry. Let her prebook your night at the Castle banquet.

Moher Lodge
Mary Considine
Cliffs of Moher
Liscannor, County Clare
Telephone: 065-7081269, 065-7081589
E-mail: moherlodge@eircom.net
Bedrooms: 4, all with private baths
Rates: €30 p.p. Discount for children negotiable. Vouchers accepted.
Credit cards: None. **Open:** April 1 to November 1. **Children:** Yes, all ages. **Pets:** No. **Smoking:** No. **Provisions for handicapped:** Yes, as far as possible. **Directions:** 3 km from Liscannor village on the R478. 1.5 km from the Cliffs of Moher.

This is a beautiful seaside dormer style modern home with pretty front garden, part of a mixed working farm with comfortable en suite triple and twin/double rooms, a lounge with warm peat fire and television. Breathtaking views and fresh air found in this seacoast region will renew your spirits. A breakfast menu is offered to guests. Nearby is renowned golf course at Lahinlir. Also, pitch and put course is available for less ambitious golfers. Additionally, there is horse riding and pony trekking. Of course a trip to the Cliffs of Moher for spectacular views is a must. That first step is a long way down. For the side trippers, go farther north a short distance and investigate the unusual geologic formation of the Burren(Burren National Park) and its unique ecology, a must for the naturalist, plus include a visit to the megalithic tombs. Mary can direct you. After your late afternoon walk or hike, a stop at a local pub will cap the day's pleasure. Don't forget to bring your camera for the scenery of this region is outstanding!

ALSO RECOMMENDED

Corofin, *Burren Lodge,* Rita Kierce, Kilnaboy. Telephone: 065-6837143. 3 bedrooms, 2 en suite. Spacious house with Burren countryside views on R476. Convenient to Lake District and Burren National Park. Dinner available. Recommended by Mary Considine of Liscannor, County Clare.

Doolin, *Churchfield,* Maeve Fitzgerald. Telephone: 065-7074209. Bedrooms: 6, 5 en suite, 1 shared. Panoramic view of Cliffs of Moher, sea, and countryside. At bus stop in Doolin. Recommended by Carmel O'Halloran of Galway. Member Town and Country Home Association.

Ennis, *Hazeldene House,* Mrs. Ina Troy, Barefields. Telephone: 065-6827212. Bedrooms: 4, all en suite with television. Private parking. Evening meals available. Modern country home on Ennis-Galway road (N18). It's 5 minutes from Ennis Center. Ideal touring base for the Burren, Cliffs of Moher, and Aillwee Caves.

Ennis, *Villa Nova,* Mrs. Mareaid O'Connor, 1 Woodlawn, Lahinch Road. Telephone: 065-6828570. Bedrooms: 5, 3 with private baths. Vouchers accepted. Bungalow on N85. Restaurant and pub with music are a 2 minutes' walk.

Lahinch, *Mulcarr House,* Mrs. Brid Fawl, Ennistymon Road. Telephone: 065-7081123. Bedrooms: 4, 3 private baths. Walking distance to golf and beach. Vouchers accepted. Smoke-free home.

County Cork

County Cork makes up almost half of Southwest Ireland, so as you can guess, there are vast differences in the terrain. In the north around Mallow, the pastureland is flat and broad with dark-green, low shrubs separating the sheep enclosures. Purple mountains can be seen to the north and west.

Moving south you will come to the town of Blarney first, with its famed Blarney Woolen Mills and the Blarney Castle, which contains the celebrated Blarney Stone. The Blarney Park Hotel nearly always has some kind of Irish music, modern or traditional, along with step dancing or set dancing to watch. Just five or six miles southeast you may visit the largest city of the Southwest, which is Cork City. Most of it sits between the north and south channels of the split Lee River, with its numerous bridges.

Here you may want to take the traditional walk along Patrick Street to the Grand Parade or wander to the edges of the city to catch glimpses of St. Mary's Pro-Cathedral or St. Finn Barre's Cathedral, the Church of St. Peter and St. Paul, or Father Matthew Memorial Church. Peruse the many art galleries and craft centers, museums, and the Cork Opera House, which offers delightful plays, musicals, and operas. We had an excellent meal in the dining room of The Moore's Hotel on Morrison's Island at the south end of town. One memorable night we walked into a small, dark, well-visited pub called "An Bodhran," and found a well-loved young fiddler playing his heart out with other musicians. He played for hours, to our joy. In September and October, look for the famous Cork Film Festival and the Jazz Festival.

Due west of Cork City on the N22 headed towards Killarney and just before a mountain pass is the beautiful medieval town of Macroom, set out in the country. Flowered window boxes abound and an old stone fort graces the town center.

About 16 miles southwest of Cork is the happy seaside town of Kinsale, labeled the Gourmet Capital of Ireland. We just missed a big gourmet competition among the many fine restaurants there on our last visit. It has the good gift shops and coffee shops of a tourist town, but a small place where we had the best soup and sandwich by a peat fire is Mother Hubbard's on Pearse Street.

From here you might want to head out to West Cork on windy little roads along tiny bays that cut into the whole of the Southwest. You'll pass beautiful small villages like Courtmacsherry, Clonakilty, Rosscarberry, and Baltimore, tucked around harbors full of sailboats. On the N71 is the classy town of Skibbereen, which booms in summer; farther west, then north, is Bantry with more formality and sophistication, and a commanding view from its hills of Bantry Bay and the wonderful mountains of the Beara Peninsula beyond.

To the east of Cork city, you'll want to see the charming port of Cobh (pronounced "Cove"), from where most emigrants had to leave by boat in the 1800s for the foreign shores of America. Imposing St. Colman's Cathedral reigns on a hill overlooking the town with its multicolored buildings fronting the harbor. Farther east is the medieval town of Youghal, with remnants of an old town gate and walls, and ancient buildings where Cromwell hid his arms. It has a pretty old lighthouse and farms that stretch out with views of the sea.

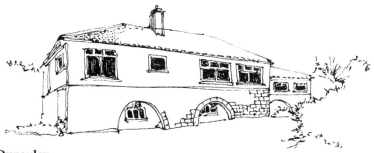

Dunauley
Rosemary McAuley
Seskin
Bantry, County Cork
Telephone and **Fax:** 027-50290
E-mail: rosemarymcauley@eircom.net
Web: www.dunauley.com
Bedrooms: 5, all with private baths. 1 self-catering suite.
Rates: €32 to 45 p.p. private bath. €45 p.p. suite; €20 for third person. 20 percent discount for children. Vouchers not accepted. **Credit cards:** None. **Open:** May 1 to September 30. **Children:** Yes, 12 or older. **Pets:** No. **Smoking:** Restricted. **Provisions for handicapped:** Yes, limited, inquire first. **Directions:** Go through town centre up a slight hill past library (big, black waterwheel turns outside library). Pass the church on right. After church, take second right, sign-posted from there. The B&B is the third house on the right. The main entry door is at the back, but car parking is provided in front once unloaded.

This modern country home is elegant and the large, comfortable living room/dining room with fireplace has wraparound bay windows with a most extraordinary panoramic view of all of Bantry Bay and the Beara Peninsula from high atop the hill. The bedrooms are very pretty and spacious. One suite of rooms downstairs is available for self-catering or long rental. All are tastefully decorated in blue, pink and green, or apricot. One of the downstairs rooms is the honeymoon bedroom. All rooms have tea- and coffee-making facilities. The breakfast menu almost defies description as it excels in most categories from fresh-squeezed orange juice or grapefruit decorated with kiwi fruit, to a trolley of cereals with toppings of raisins and fruit, to omelets with 4 fillings, or smoked salmon and scrambled eggs. Brewed coffee and a variety of teas complement the entrées, not to mention the scones and homemade breads. Extraordinary! Fishing, sailing, golf, walks, and Bantry House are in town 5 minutes away.

Larchwood House
Sheila Vaughan
Pearsons Bridge
Bantry, County Cork
Telephone: 027-66181
Bedrooms: 4, all private baths
Rates: € 40 p.p. Vouchers not accepted. €36 dinner. **Credit cards**:
VISA, AMEX, MasterCard, Diners. **Open**: All year. **Children**: Yes, all
ages. **Pets**: No. **Smoking**: Limited. **Provisions for handicapped**: None.
Directions: On the N71 at Ballylickey, take Kealkill Road for 2 miles,
north of Bantry. At Pearsons Bridge on Kealkill Road, take a sharp
right. The house is 300 yards on the right.

A rare find is this enchanting "restaurant with rooms." The B&B is
part of a small, intimate gourmet restaurant with cooking that has
flair and originality. The bedrooms are luxurious, spacious, and beautifully decorated. The dining room overlooks their grand gardens and
a small river. For those who like exquisite dining and then a peaceful
evening in an elegant bedroom upstairs—instead of a lot of driving—
this is the place. The gardens are the handiwork of the husband,
Aiden Vaughan, a professional photographer, who has transformed
the surroundings, using stone and plants, into an extraordinary,
enchanting 6 acres of beauty. Sheila matches his artistry in the culi-
nary department. Breakfast is ordered off a menu and features fresh
fruit; eggs any style, some with smoked salmon (typically Irish) or
grilled kippered herring; baked fresh haddock; and a local cheese
plate. She has been a super chef at the Dromoland Castle. The small
lounge provides drinks in a homey atmosphere, or you can take a
stroll through the garden down the "39 steps" to a place where the
local salmon river becomes a pool. The Vaughans are gracious and
will make this an idyllic treat off the beaten path. Golf, horseback
riding, fishing, sailing, and walking paths are also nearby.

Shangri-la
Ursula Schiesser
Glengarriff Road
Bantry, County Cork
Telephone: 027-50244
Fax: 027-50244
E-mail: schiesserbb@eircom.net
Bedrooms: 6; all with private baths
Rates: €28 p.p. private bath; Single €38.50; 25 percent discount for children under 10. Vouchers accepted. €18 dinner. **Credit cards:** VISA and MasterCard. **Open:** February 1 to November 15. **Children:** All ages. **Pets:** No. **Smoking:** Restricted. **Provisions for handicapped:** No, hillside lot. **Directions:** Coming from Cork on the N71, the Glengarriff Road, take the first right after ROWA Pharmaceuticals and the first left to enter the car park at the back of the property.

The view from the living room and sun porch is panoramic and beautiful. The rooms are handsomely decorated: one in green and aqua flowers, one with a pink and white canopy, another with an orange and lace canopy. All are fashionable, charming, and comfortable, with coffee- and tea-making facilities, hair dryers, and television. Ms. Schiesser is a delightful host and will make your stay in Bantry a pleasant one. We were enchanted with the story of the first settlers in Ireland, who came ashore in Bantry led by Cessera, a woman captaining the crew of 53. Ask her about the soup field across the street. There is a choice of menu for breakfast. Some different choices are coddled eggs and pancakes as well as cheeses, fruits, and yogurts. The full Irish Breakfast is served in the pretty dining room adjoining the well-appointed living room. All common rooms have views of the water and the garden. Many rooms also have a view of the water. This B&B maintains high standards! Bantry House and Gardens and fishing, sailing, walks, and golf are in the area. In 1996, there will be a bicentennial celebration of the French Armada in Bantry Bay.

Claragh Bed and Breakfast
Cecilia Kiely
Waterloo Road, Garrycloyne
Blarney, County Cork
Telephone and **Fax:** 021-4886308
E-mail: claraghbandb@eircom.net
Web: www.claragh.com
Bedrooms: 4, with private bath
Rates: €26-28 p.p. private bath. 10 percent discount for children.
Vouchers accepted. **Credit cards:** VISA and MasterCard. **Open:** April 1 to
October 31. **Children:** Yes, ages 9 and up. **Pets:** No. **Smoking:** No. **Provisions for handicapped:** Yes, room with 1 double bed, 1 single bed. **Directions:** Follow signs on Waterloo Road out of Blarney Village to Claragh.
About 2 miles out, you'll find the house on the left. Waterloo Road is
200 yards past Blarney Woolen Mills on left (going toward Cork City).

Cecilia Kiely will surely lighten your visit to the Irish Republic with
her boundless energy and special Irish humor and she makes your visit
especially warm and friendly with her care in directing you to the sights
and sounds of Blarney and Cork City. Electric blankets are turned on
before you retire. The lovely lounge offers tea and coffee facilities and has
a fireplace. The dining room allows for separate tables. The bedrooms
are decorated in pink and green, and peach and green with floral
accents. All have television, hair dryers, and tea/coffee facilities. Breakfast
has fresh homemade brown bread, scones, fresh fruit salad, and yogurts
along with a choice of cooked Irish Breakfast. Cecilia features a French
toast with syrup and a cinnamon applesauce that is delicious. This charming one-floor home is set in tranquil gardens in a historic area. The estate
was once owned by Equerry to the Prince of Wales. This home is near
Blarney Woolen Mills and other shops. You can kiss the Blarney Stone at
the castle, hear Irish music, dance traditional Irish set dances, or swim at
Blarney Park Hotel. You may want to try to catch the big salmon, as Frank
did (tried, that is) Check out Christie's Restaurant. It's great! The new
River Martin Valley Walk is near, so guests can walk 1.5 miles to town.

Inchavara House
Breda O'Dwyer
Stoneview
Blarney, County Cork
Telephone: 021-4385549
E-mail: bridiegirlie@yahoo.com
Bedrooms: 4; 3 with private baths; 1 shared
Rates: €32 p.p. private bath; Shared €30. Vouchers not accepted.
Credit cards: None. **Open:** April 1 to November 1. **Children:** 7 and up.
Pets: No. **Smoking:** No. **Provisions for handicapped:** None. **Directions:**
From N20, exit on R617 to Blarney Village. After Blarney Filling Station, follow signs for house on right. Stay on road 2 km to first crossroad and turn left. You will see signs for Inchavara. It over looks village.

This lovely country home was recommended to us by a guest in Dublin, and again by another B&B owner in Blarney, and we are thrilled to include it. What a delightful home, with a beautiful dining room and spacious television lounge, both opening to a large conservatory or sun room with floor-to-ceiling glass, overlooking the beautiful garden in front and hills and Blarney Castle beyond. Tea and coffee facilities are available all day. It is a great place for having a before-dinner drink or playing cards. The bedrooms are decorated in blues and pinks. One bedroom with a huge bath is very large, fitted with a double and a single brass bed. Mrs. O'Dwyer is a congenial and welcoming host. The breakfast is regular or continental. The regular breakfast includes a choice of eggs, black pudding, and hot scones to name a few extras. The buffet of cereals, yogurts, and fruits makes a nice continental one. The coffee is brewed! Horseback riding and golf can be found nearby in Blarney, and there are lovely walks in this area.

Knockawn Wood
Ita and Fergus O'Donovan
Curraleigh
Inniscara
Blarney, County Cork
Telephone and **Fax**: 021-4870284
E-mail: odknkwd@iol.ie
Bedrooms: 4, 3 with private bath, 1 shared
Rates: €28 p.p. private bath; €25 p.p. shared bath; 50 percent discount for children. Vouchers accepted. Dinner €17. **Credit cards:** VISA and Access. **Open:** January 1 to December 31. **Children:** All ages. **Pets:** No. **Smoking:** Restricted. **Provisions for handicapped:** None. **Directions:** From Blarney (6 miles away), follow Killarney signs on R618. From Cork, take N22 for 3 miles, then turn right onto R618 for 5 miles.

If you need a lodging easily accessible to Cork City and Blarney, this is a good choice. Ita and Fergus will make your stay in the area a pleasant one. Tea and scones are offered on arrival, also you can request a delicious dinner for the evening meal while you're settling in. Their quiet, picturesque setting in the country and their experience in the hospitality profession(Ita managed hotels) will take care of your every need. Even babysitting is provided. Bedrooms are done in blues, pinks and green and cream combinations. Tea/coffee facilities and television in rooms. A comfortable lounge with bright lemon decor has sparkling chandelier and corniced ceiling. The breakfast menu is quite extensive, starting with juices and fresh fruit, followed by a variety of hot and cold cereals. The main course has a full Irish plate plus extras like tomatoes, mushrooms, and beans, or pancakes with syrup. Nearby is salmon fishing on the Lee River and course angling on Inniscarra Lakes. Cork airport and ferry are 30 minutes away. Horse riding and walking available by lake and woods.

Hillside Farm
Bella Helen
Kilgarriffe
Clonakilty, County Cork
Telephone: 023-33139
E-mail: richardhelen@eircom.net
Bedrooms: 4; 2 with private baths, 2 with shared
Rates: €29 p.p. private bath; €26 shared bath; 50 percent discount for
children. Vouchers accepted. €15 dinner. **Credit cards:** None. **Open:**
May to October. **Children:** All ages. **Pets:** Yes. **Smoking:** No. **Provisions
for handicapped:** None. **Directions:** To the northwest from Cork, turn
right at the Shell station onto Enniskeane Road (R588). The farm is 4
km on the left. It is a 45-minute drive from Cork Airport.

When we were there, pups were being born in the hayloft, new
calves were suckling their mothers, chickens, geese, and rare fowl
were clucking and calling in the barnyard. This is a 150-acre, living,
vibrant dairy farm with all the noises and smells one would expect at
a rural homestead. Mrs. Helen served us fresh scones with her own
crab-apple jelly (just made) on the side shelf of her old-style kitchen.
She gives baking demonstrations. Although rustic, this pink farmhouse B&B has appeal for those who like to visit a working farm.
There are fine views from beautifully furnished rooms. The comfortable lounge has antique furniture, and the dining room is attractive.
Dinner features 4 courses, with a roast such as leg of lamb or salmon,
potato, fresh brown bread, 2 vegetables from the garden, and berry
pie. Yum! Breakfast is likewise scrumptious and generous with homemade white pudding, jams, and jellies. It is a great place for young
children to learn about farm life. They would never want to leave.
This farm is within 45 minutes' drive of Cork Airport and Ringaskiddy
Ferryport. There is good bird watching along the estuary. Look for
the ancient Temple Bryan and the Lisnagun Stone.

Belvedere Lodge
Tim and Marie McGrath
Tivoli
Cork City, County Cork
Telephone and **Fax:** 021-4501682
E-mail: info@belvederelodge.com
Web: www.belvederelodge.com
Bedrooms: 20, all with private baths
Rates: €50-60. Vouchers not accepted. Children's discount 50 percent.
Credit cards: All major ones. **Open:** January 2 to December 22. **Children:** Yes, all ages. **Pets:** Only guide dogs. **Smoking:** Yes. **Provisions for handicapped:** Yes. **Directions:** One mile east of Cork City on Rosslare/Dublin road just 100 yards past service stations on left. Belvedere is 200 yards before Silver Springs Hotel.

This lovely Victorian guesthouse with a unique wrought-iron veranda has spacious, beautifully decorated bedrooms and nine new luxury rooms. The elegant curtains and quilts and wall to wall carpeting in the bedrooms. Colors are two-tone rose, apricot, or turquoise. One room has a bay window with seats; one has a slinding glass door to the garden. They all have televisions, telephones, and tea and coffee makers. The beautiful lounge is light cranberry with a Victorian floral decor, a marble fireplace, and accompanying period furniture. The equally handsome dining room is light cranberry with green carpeting with separate tables, all adjoining the patio with a view of the garden. An elaborate breakfast menu includes selection of fresh fruits, fresh-squeezed orange juice, a selection of cereals, fresh fish and grills, and scrambled eggs with smoked salmon. There is a private secure car park. The Belvedere Lodge offers a good base for visiting the sights in Cork, Blarney, Kinsale, and may historical and cultural sights. The McGraths can direct you to the recreational facilities and restaurants.

Cois Coille
Rita Barry-Murphy
Glengariff, County Cork
Telephone: 027-63202
Web: www.coiscoille.com
Bedrooms: 6 with private baths
Rates: €30 p.p.; 20 percent discount for children. Vouchers not accepted. **Credit cards:** None. **Open:** March 14 to November 16. **Children:** All ages. **Pets:** No. **Smoking:** No. **Provisions for handicapped:** None. **Directions:** Sign posted on Bantry Road, 100 meters from Eccles Hotel, overlooking Glengariff Harbour.

Cois Coille is a lovely, modern, dormered home in an award-winning terraced, riverside garden, on a hill overlooking Bantry Bay. It is a comfortable country home in a quiet neighborhood. The rooms are beautifully decorated in pinks and greens and designed to be pleasant to the eye. All have tea/coffee facilities. Some have panoramic harbor views; one has its own private patio. The television lounge and dining room both enjoy mountain and garden views. Rita offers an extensive breakfast menu, featuring an Irish "Fry" or scrambled, boiled, or poached eggs, fresh fruit plate and yogurt, Irish cheese, baked beans or smoked salmon or herring, homemade breads, scones, and preserves, fresh-squeezed orange juice, and fresh-brewed coffee. Golfing, boating, fishing, scenic walks, and horseback riding are available in the area. Tour the famous Beara Penninsula with ferries to Clear Island. Exotic Garnish Island Gardens are only 10 minutes away. Irish is spoken here.

Chart House
Billy and Mary O'Connor
6 Denis Quay
Kinsale, County Cork
Telephone: 021-4774568
Fax: 021-4777907
E-mail: charthouse@eircom.net
Bedrooms: 4 with private baths
Rates: 45-76 p.p. **Credit cards:** Yes. **Open:** All year except Christmas.
Children: No. **Pets:** No. **Smoking:** No. **Provisions for handicapped:**
None. **Directions:** In the street (Denis Quay) between the Trident and
Actons Hotels, turn right after Actons. Chart House is the last on the
right.

Chart House is an elegant two-hundred-year-old family-run Georgian house in Ireland's oldest town. Beautifully furnished with
antique beds, orthopedic mattresses, snowy white linens, and handsome spreads, it has luxurious stately bathrooms with power showers
and Jacuzzi whirlpool baths. All rooms have a telephone, satellite television, hair dryer, and iron press. Two fine rooms are blue and green.
One standard double is done in pink, and a small single room is
painted in a cream color. Breakfast is served at a long mahogany table
in their elegant light-green and white dining room. You will find cereals, fruit, nuts and yogurt, homemade scones, brown bread, and
muffins. A full Irish with Clonakilty black-and-white pudding is served
along with pan-fried mushrooms on toast, or scrambled egg with
smoked salmon, or omelets, or other types of eggs, and organic porridge made with a touch of Irish Mist. This house is within walking distance of a yachting club marina, and is an easy 2-minute walk to
Kinsale's many gourmet restaurants. Old Head Golf Links, sailing,
horse riding, and scenic walks are close by.

The Lighthouse
Carmel Kelly-O'Gorman
The Rock
Kinsale, County Cork
Telephone: 021-4772734
Fax: 021-4773282
E-mail: info@lighthouse-kinsale.com
Web: www.lighthouse-kinsale.com
Bedrooms: 5, all with private baths
Rates: €50-55 p.p.; Single €80; 25 percent discount for children.
Vouchers not accepted. **Credit cards:** VISA, MasterCard, Access,
AmEx. **Open:** All year. **Children:** Yes, 10 and older. **Pets:** No. **Smoking:** Restricted. **Provisions for handicapped:** None. **Directions:** Take
R600 to town. At the White House Hotel, bear left; follow the white
line for 2 minutes (⅓ mile) until you reach the sign for the community
school. Go right and follow the white line to the top of road. You'll
see a sign post for a lighthouse. The home is up short, steep hill on
right. It is a Tudor house with an old in sign.

This elegant bed and breakfast was built on the site of the old
Kinsale Beacon. It has been completely renovated since the fire of
1993. Carmel, an interior decorator among other things, fashioned
a B&B with a touch of class and refinement. Every room is
appointed with antiques. One private suite has its own sitting room.
The four-poster and canopy beds in the Georgian suite or the
Empire room are beautiful. The Victorian dining room is in
Regency style with old prints of London that provide a perfect
match for the period decor. Breakfast features a choice of juices
or raspberries in champagne, cereals (including honey muesli),
yogurts, fancy teas, smoked salmon and scrambled eggs, Irish cheddar and other cheeses, black and white puddings, mushrooms, kippers with lemon butter, and so on. You will certainly have your fill
of Irish delicacies. Carmel will lead you to the best restaurants and
make your visit to Kinsale, the Irish gourmet capital, a highlight of
your trip. Her B&B is within reach of shark fishing, yacht rental,
world championship Old Head Golf Links, and three riding stables.

Rivermount House
Claire O'Sullivan
Knocknabinny, Barrells Cross
Kinsale, County Cork
Telephone: 021-4778033
Fax: 021-4778225
E-mail: rivermnt@iol.ie
Bedrooms: 6, all with private baths
Rates: €30-35 p.p.; 10 percent discount for children. Vouchers accepted. Dinner offered. **Credit cards:** VISA/MasterCard. **Open:** February 1 to December 1. **Children:** All ages. **Pets:** No. **Smoking:** No. **Provisions for handicapped:** No. **Directions:** Continue on R600 through Kinsale to the Old Head. Go over bridge. Turn right. Continue on 1.5 km to large crossroad. Turn right. Rivermount is fourth house on right. It is 4 km from Kinsale on road to Ballinspittle.

This large lovely modern, country home situated on a four acre lot in quiet setting with spectacular views of the Brandon River has a great deal of charm and character. There are many amenities such as: baby-sitting, televisions and tea/coffee makers, telephones, radios, hair dryers, and private off-street parking. The bedrooms are pink with matching fabrics, the large lounge has warm red walls and green carpeting, and the bright and airy conservatory is yellow and green. A luxurious decor exists throughout the whole house and is obvious the minute you enter. The breakfast is varied from traditional to salmon or pancakes, the emphasis is on home produce.Nearby there is sailing (Kinsale is one of the largest recreational sailing centers in all of Ireland), fishing, beaches, and horseback riding. Also, Kinsale hosts a gourmet restaurant festival in the fall, but you will find good eating here any time of the year, There are many quaint and extraordinary restaurants where you find gourmet and country fare served in varied ambiences. The Old Head golf club is nearby.

Walyunga
Myrtle Levis
Sandycove
Kinsale, County Cork
Telephone and **Fax:** 021-4774126
E-mail: info@walyunga.com
Bedrooms: 5; 4 with private baths, 1 with shared
Rates: € 29-38 p.p. private; €25-29 p.p. shared. 25 percent discount
for children under 12. **Credit cards:** VISA. **Open:** March to end of
October. **Children:** Yes, 5 or older. **Pets:** No. **Smoking:** No. **Provisions
for handicapped:** None. **Directions:** From the Trident Hotel in Kin-
sale, follow the Sandycove signs west across the long bridge. As you
approach Sandycove signs, you will see the Walyunga sign. Walyunga
is about 2 miles from Trident Hotel. Follow sign posts.

This pleasant couple offers a modern country home with hanging
plants and a feeling of openness to nature by a creative use of glass
and skylights. There are grand views of the Atlantic Ocean with a lighthouse in the distance through large picture windows. A sliding glass
door in front opens to a garden and meadow. Mr. Levis, an elemen-
tary-school teacher, knows the natural history of the region, and gives
advice on genealogical quests. They had spent many years in Australia,
thus the name Walyunga. All rooms are modern and spacious with
fluffy quilts. One is a front corner room with a large bed and spacious
bath that we took to be the "honeymoon suite." The pastel colors in the
rooms with fine furniture and woodwork make this an attractive home.
The sun was brilliant when we were there, and the delicious breakfast
with brewed coffee and a view out the front was memorable. They offer
a variety of cereals, porridge, fruit salad, yogurt, smoked salmon, scrambled egg in addition to an Irish Breakfast. Nearby are sandy beaches,
fishing, boating, and scenic coastal walks. Walyuuga is en route to the
internationally acclaimed Old Head of Kinsale golf links.

Ballymakeigh House
Margaret Browne
Killeagh
Youghal, County Cork
Telephone: 024-95184
Fax: 024-95370
E-mail: ballymakeigh@eircom.net
Bedrooms: 6, all with private baths
Rates: €50 p.p.; Single €60. Vouchers not accepted. €35 for dinner.
Credit cards: Visa, MasterCard, Access. **Open:** February 1 to October 30. **Children:** All ages. **Pets:** Negotiable. **Smoking:** Restricted. **Provisions for handicapped:** None. **Directions:** House is 22 miles east of Cork City, off the N25. Go straight between Old Thatch Pub (where there is a sign for Ballymakeigh House) and the church in Killeagh when turning off the N25. Their driveway is on the right about a ½ mile.

This stately and refined eighteenth-century farmhouse, elegantly decorated by Mrs. Browne, is a showpiece for decor and colors. The Brownes were the 1992 winners of the A.I.B./I.F.J. Agri-Tourism National Award for Best Farmhouse B&B. In 1997 she won the A. A. Land Lady of the Year Award. There is a glassed-in conservatory for lounging and teas. The bedrooms are spacious with charming views of the meadows. They have extras like French soap, facecloths, hair dryers, and suitcase racks. All bedrooms newly decorated in pastel shades. The dining room is done in green and red with an antique piano. Fresh flowers abound. Gourmet cooking by your host will delight your palate both at breakfast and at dinner. For breakfast you get a choice of free-range eggs, porridge, fresh orange juice, grapefruit or apple juice. Kippers are offered too. Tennis courts are on the grounds. They also have a game room and play area. Ballymakeigh has opened its equestrian centre for all levels of riders. Michael drives guests to their new restaurant now. Three golf courses are nearby and the house is convenient to Midleton Heritage Park, Fota, Trabolgan, Vee, Blarney, Cork Airport and Ferryport, Ballymaloe, and sandy beaches.

ALSO RECOMMENDED

Blarney, *The White House,* Pat and Regina Coughlin, Blarney Town. Telephone: 021-4385338. Bedrooms: 6 with private baths. ½ mile from Blarney Center on the Mallow road.

Clonakilty, *Ard Na Greine,* Norma Walsh, Balinascarthy. Telelphone: 023-39104. Fax: 023-39397. Bedrooms: 6, 4 en suite. Farm B&B. 6 km from Clonakilty on N71. Dinner available. Won Galtee Breakfast Award. Recommended by many travel guides. Spectacular view of countryside. E-mail Norma Walsh at normawalsh1@eircom.net

Gourgane Barra, *Gourgane Barra Hotel,* Christopher and Breda Lucey, Ballingeary. Telephone: 026-47069/47223. Fax: 026-47226. Bedrooms: 28, all with private baths. Lovely guesthouse on its own grounds tucked away in beautiful mountains of West Cork. Inland from Glengarriff, overlooking Gougane Barra Lake, the source of the Lee River. Family-owned-and-operated hotel. The favorite of Dan Callanan of Beverly Cove, Mass.

Kinsale, *Hillside House,* Margaret Griffin, Camp-Hill, on the hill above Kinsale Town. Telephone: 021-4772315. Bedrooms: 6 with private baths. Open: January 7 to December 20. Beautiful sea view. Conservatory.

COUNTY DONEGAL

County Donegal

County Donegal, way up in the northwest corner of Ireland, has a definite rugged character all its own. Settlers came here in 7000 b.c. It doesn't seem to suffer from being almost entirely bordered on the east by Northern Ireland. You could spend a week or two there and not see all the wonderful and varied sights. To the northwest, it is very mountainous, and the N56 takes you on a grand tour of the seacoast with its hundreds of inlets and wonderful fishing villages on the Atlantic Ocean. You'll find great rock formations and fine sandy beaches for swimming and surfing.

If you decide to travel up the eastern side of Lough Swilly to see the ancient ruins and castles of the spectacular Inishowen Peninsula, the R38 makes a circular tour. This area was settled by Normans in the tenth century.

Letterkenny seems to be the most central city for all these trips and it's a fun town to visit on its own. Tourist Information is on Derry Road and open June to September. The majestic St. Euman's Cathedral is especially pretty lit up at night. Visit the Donegal County Museum on High Road, and choose from a number of good pubs downtown almost any night in summer for singalongs and traditional Irish music. Two good restaurants are the Gleneany House and The Silver Tassie in Letterkenny. Golf, fishing, and swimming are very close at hand. From here it's only 30 minutes northwest to the unspoiled wildness of Glenveagh National Park, with its Castle and Gardens on 25,000 acres and beautiful, dramatic views of mountains, rivers, and vales. Letterkenny is a good home base for a trip around to the Antrim coast, with the peculiar, enormous, step-rock formation called the Giant's Causeway. It's a quick ride to the thriving, exciting town of Derry, too. Try the excellent DaVinci's Restaurant for atmosphere and great choices. On the way, through Carrigans, in eastern Donegal, you'll find charming country scenes and vistas, a photographer's dream.

To the south is the lovely Lough Eske and Donegal, a small town with charm, great for shopping and trying dinners in good hotels and restaurants. You'll find handcrafted woolen goods and Donegal tweeds for sale in the shops. Donegal Castle is a walk from the Diamond in the center of town. Ask where the good Irish music is playing in lounges and pubs. It's very popular there. Hyland Central Hotel has a good Sunday Buffet.

Travel out west of Donegal on the N15 to Killybegs, with its fishing fleet. When we were in County Wexford, clear across the country, we met a man who said he traveled every week to fish on his boat out of Killybegs, as the fishing is so good there. It's a pleasant drive north to the fishing villages of Portnoo, Ardara, and Glencolumbkille, with its Folk Park, all on the Atlantic Ocean.

Ballyshannon is the southern gateway to Donegal County. It has a musical Folk Festival every July or August. Visit Beleek with its delicate pottery, just a few miles away on the Fermanagh border and visit the neat beaches of Rossnowlagh, where you can surf or water-ski.

Cavangarden House
Agnes McCaffrey
Ballyshannon, County Donegal
Telephone: 072-51365
E-mail: cghouse@iol.ie
Bedrooms: 6, all with private baths
Rates: €27 p.p.; 33 percent discount for children. Vouchers accepted.
€19 dinner on request. **Credit cards:** VISA, MasterCard, AmEx. **Open:**
All year except Christmas. **Children:** All ages. **Pets:** No. **Smoking:** No.
Provisions for handicapped: Yes, one ground-floor room. **Other features:** Plenty of parking. **Directions:** The house is 11 miles south of
Donegal Town on the N15 on the right, or 3 miles north of Ballyshannon on the left.

We drove down a country lane with sheep and cows grazing on
either side and came to a stately 1750 stucco manor house. Mrs. McCaffrey graciously served us tea in the classically decorated, high-ceilinged
living room, by the marble fireplace. Antique gold-framed mirrors and
pictures graced the walls and a conversation piece was a fancy lounge
couch covered in caramel-colored velvet. The rooms were a surprise
with oversized antique mahogany beds, comfy quilts, and handsome
dark bureaus and tables. Walls all have large-floral-printed paper, Victorian style. The two rooms on the third floor are more modern and
sunny with skylights. Pastoral scenes and bright green hills can be seen
from each room. Cavangarden House reminded us of a grand old
house we stayed at in Limoges, France. The castle-sized dining room
has a very long, dark, wood table and carved-back chairs. Beside the
Irish Breakfast, Mrs. McCaffrey serves yogurt and fruit and features delicious homemade scones. Rossnowlagh Beach is 3 miles away with swimming and windsurfing and the house is quite near to Donegal Town.

Mount Royd
Josephine Martin
Carrigans (near Derry), County Donegal
Telephone: 074-40163
Fax: 074-40400
E-mail: jmartin@mountroyd.com
Bedrooms: 4, all with private baths
Rates: €27-28 p.p.; Single €38.80. Vouchers accepted. Dinner offered.
Credit cards: None. **Open:** All year. **Children:** Yes, 10 and up. **Pets:** Yes. **Smoking:** Restricted. **Provisions for handicapped:** Yes, 1 room.
Directions: Carrigans has signs posted on the N13 and N14. From Derry City, take Letterkenny Road (A40) and stay on A40 to Carrigans. Mount Royd is on left. From Letterkenny, take N13 until you see signs for Carrigans.

This elegant 50-year-old Georgian country home is one of our favorites because of the pastoral setting and the extraordinary care that Mrs. Martin has taken in decorating and furnishing her spacious home. It was a farmhouse and they still have sheep grazing in the meadows of their 12 acres. Your hostess greets you with tea and her special apricot or nut scones, and shows you a video of the highlights of the region in the cozy living room in front of the fire. Recently she has won the RAC "Little Gem" Award and was a finalist in AA's Laudlady of the Year in 2001. The guest rooms are all large and very lovely with lots of ruffles in varying shades of pink, blue, or peach. Laura Ashley printed quilts grace the beds and each large bath has fancy colored soaps matching Mrs. Martin's theme. The pink room has a butterfly theme. One bedroom is pink and rose and has a fireplace. The breakfast is served in her handsome dining room with a trolley of apricots, grapefruit, and mandarin oranges, fresh fluffy scones, and home-baked currant bread in addition to a choice of omelet or fried eggs, bacon and sausage, or yogurt, cheese, and cereal. The Martins love to tell of Agatha Christie living and writing her mysteries in a big house just across the road. Derry is only five miles away, where you can eat DaVinci's or the Old Church Restaurant nearby. Tour the Inishowen Peninsula, Londonderry, and the fascinating Giant's Causeway on the coast of Antrim. Also 5 miles away is the Cavanacor Historic House and Craft Center, the ancestral home of U.S. President James Polk. A historic fort, Grianin of Aileach, is nearby, too.

Ardeevin
Mary McGinty
Lough Eske, Barnesmore
Donegal Town, County Donegal
Telephone and **Fax:** 073-21790
E-mail: seanmcginty@eircom.net
Web: members.tripod.com/~ardeevin
Bedrooms: 6 with private baths
Rates: €27.50-40 p.p. 20 percent discount for children under 12.
Vouchers accepted. **Credit cards:** None. **Open:** March to November.
Children: All ages. **Pets:** No. **Smoking:** No. **Provisions for handi-
capped:** None. **Directions:** Going south from Letterkenny on the N15,
2 miles after Biddy O'Barnes' Pub on the right, turn right. Follow
the signs down the winding country road for about 1 mile. Out of
Donegal Town, follow Derry Road (N15) for 4 km until you come to
a fork in the road. Turn left, follow the signs to Lough Eske, then follow the Ardeevin signs the rest of the way.

Mary McGinty and her husband, a charming and hospitable couple,
run this lovely B&B country home, which is newly renovated and is surrounded by the Bluestack Mountains. The bedrooms are pretty, with
flowered duvets in pinks and blues and handsome mahogany wood
headboards. All rooms, including the dining room, have an exquisite
view of Lough Eske. Tea- and coffee-making facilities are in each room.
You are close to Donegal Town. Visit McGinty's knitting shop for some
real bargains. This place is a delight because of its beautiful rooms, the
spacious dining room with lake views, and genuinely friendly hosts. The
buffet-style breakfast has a full array of delicious offerings like Kippers
and seafood crepes, but we were thrilled with the pancakes and syrup.
Other offerings were fresh fruit, yogurt, cheese and scones, and of
course the Irish Breakfast. O'Donnell Castle in town is restored and
open to the public. Harvey's Point restaurant across the lake is great.
The area is ideal for horseback riding, fishing, hiking, and golf, 8 miles
away at Rossnowlagh, and for its forests, and lakes. Winner of AA Four-
Star, RAC Four-Star, and RAC Sparkling Diamond Award.

Ardglas
Breid and Paddy Kelly
Lurgybrack, Sligo Road
Letterkenny, County Donegal
Telephone and **Fax**: 074-22516;
Email: ardglas@yahoo.co.uk
Bedrooms: 6 with private baths
Rates: €25.50 p.p. 30 percent discount for children under 12. Vouchers are accepted. **Credit cards:** VISA, Access, and MasterCard. **Open:** Easter to mid-October. **Children:** All ages. **Pets:** No. **Smoking:** Restricted. **Provisions for handicapped:** Yes. **Directions:** Take N14 out of Letterkenny; take Derry Road to Dry Arch Roundabout to the N13 (Sligo Road). Go 1 mile—the house is on the left.

This beautiful, spacious Georgian bungalow with many windows is high on a hill and some of the rooms look out onto grazing sheep and mountain views. The spacious entrance has a carved wooden staircase. Breid is most gracious as a hostess. The living room has a television, flagstone fireplace, and soft cocoa-colored chairs. All the rooms are large, with cream with turquoise rugs, and have matching duvets and curtains in flowered prints of quiet colors. The upstairs rooms are larger. All of the rooms have televisions, hair dryers, and tea-making facilities. Breid has 4 family rooms. Her Irish Breakfast includes fresh fruit, yogurt, and cereal, boiled or poached eggs, or porridge. Paddy and his son both teach woodworking in secondary schools. It is an ideal place for visiting North Donegal, Derryveigh, and Northern Ireland's wonderful seacoast. It is close to golf, fishing, bowling, walking, and horseback riding, and you'll find three cinemas as well as a leisure center with swimming in town.

Glencairn House
Maureen McCleary
Ramelton Road
Letterkenny, County Donegal
Telephone: 074-24393/ 25242
E-mail: glencairnbb@hotmail.com
Bedrooms: 6; 5 with private baths, 1 private not in room
Rates: €25.50 p.p. €23.50 shared bath. Single €36-38.50. ⅓ discount for
children under 12. Vouchers accepted. **Credit cards:** All major ones.
Open: All year except Christmas week. **Children:** All ages. **Pets:** No.
Smoking: Restricted to lounge. **Provisions for handicapped:** Rooms
on ground floor. **Directions:** Coming into Letterkenny take Ramelton
Road (R245) to the right. As you climb the hill, Glencairn House is on
your right. Drop down into the large car park. It is near Mount
Errigul Hotel.

This modern suburban home on a hillside is gorgeous. From the
etching on the front door, to the large gold and beige bathroom, to
the spacious room with a spectacular view of the whole valley—all is
beautiful! You may see the Swilly River valley from the side patio,
which has lounge chairs. The pink and green, beige and pale apricot, and grey and pink in the new decorated bedrooms give them a
soft and elegant look. All headboards are covered in velvet. Rooms
have tea/ coffee-making facilities and television. The family room on
the right is Frank's favorite. It has a double and single bed, dressing
table or desk, and large bath. The large lounge with a fireplace will be
where you are greeted with tea or coffee on your arrival. A full Irish
breakfast is served with fruit, yogurt, cheese, cereal, and porridge in
the large dining room, which has separate tables and a view. This
place is a great bargain! Golf, bowling, and three cinemas are in the
area. Ask for directions to good salmon fishing. Silvertassie Hotel
and Holiday Inn are nearby.

Radharc Na Giuise
Jennie and Jim Bradley
Kilmacrennan Road
Letterkenny, County Donegal
Telephone: 074-22090
Fax: 074-25139
E-mail: bradleybb21@hotmail.com
Bedrooms: 6, all with private baths
Rates: €25.50 p.p., single person €38.50. Children 33 percent discount. Vouchers accepted. **Credit cards:** Visa and MasterCard. **Open:** January 8 to December 20. **Children:** Yes, all ages. **Pets:** No. **Smoking:** No. **Provisions for handicapped:** None. **Directions:** Situated on the main Glenveagh National Park Road overlooking town on the N56 to Dunfanaghy. 0.5 km above hospital roundabout. Look for modern grey-stone and white home with two-windowed dormer, garden with shrubs in front and driveway on the right.

This attractive dormered bungalow overlooking the town, with pretty gardens in front and back garden for visitorÕs use, is convenient to local shops and restaurants. Jennie will give you a warm and friendly Irish welcome when you arrive, and describe the tourist highlights of Donegal if requested. The lounge is cozily decorated with fireplace for postcard writing or card playing. You have a selection of six beautifully decorated bedrooms with soft colored curtains and throwovers. Rooms are cream primrose, two yellow and lemon with green and gold curtains and green patterned rug, all with throwovers to match the decor. Each room has a television, hair dryer and tea/coffee facilities, tissues and a small flower arrangement.. Recreation in the area gives you choice of golfing, horseback riding, fishing, tennis, and go-carting. Letterkenny also has a leisure center. Jennie's bed and breakfast was a "Tidy Towns" award winner last year. She can also tell you about Riverdance, as her daughter has been a member of the troupe the last four years.

Town View B&B
May and Danny Herrity
Leck Road
Letterkenny, County Donegal
Telephone: 074-21570
E-mail: townview@eircom.net
Bedrooms: 6, all with private baths
Rates: €26 p.p. Vouchers accepted. **Credit cards:** VISA and Master-Card. **Open:** All year. **Children:** Yes, 8 or older. **Pets:** No. **Smoking:** Restricted. **Provisions for handicapped:** None. **Directions:** From the center of town, take Main Street to the foot of the hill to Dunnes Store. Go left, cross over the bridge, and stay left for ½ mile. Follow the signs to the B&B, or call owner from town.

A modern, white-stucco bungalow, this B&B has pleasantly comfortable rooms all decorated in pastel blues and geens. May is a great hostess, serving you tea on arrival and leading you on a good tour around the area. The view of the whole town from her sitting room is spectacular by day or night. Beautiful lamps and antiques adorn the house and the dining room is also spacious with views. Breakfast is a gourmet delight with a buffet of lots of fruits, cereals, yogurts and cheeses in addition to her full cooked Irish Breakfast. She has won a Galtee award for her good breakfasts. Danny and her son and daughter help with the work; Dan has a horse of his own in a little barn. A large car park is available, and golf, ten-pin bowling, and a swimming pool are open to visitors of Letterkenny town. They are close to the famous Glenveagh Castle and Gardens, and Rathmullen Beach. One night we drove to Derry for an excellent dinner. Horseback riding, golf, fishing, and hill walking are nearby.

Thalassa Country Home
Eva Friel
Narin
Portnoo, County Donegal
Telephone: 075-45151
Bedrooms: 4, all with private baths
Rates: €28 p.p. 25 percent discount for children under 12. Vouchers accepted. €17 dinner. **Credit cards:** VISA. **Open:** February to November. **Children:** All ages. **Pets:** No. **Smoking:** Restricted. **Provisions for handicapped:** None. **Directions:** Take the N56 to Ardara, then R261 to Portnoo-Narin, about 5 km. Follow the sign for Portnoo. The house is on the coast road overlooking the ocean and golf course. Look for Thalassa signs.

If ocean views are your choice, this modern country home will provide you with plenty of breathtaking scenery in this beautiful part of Donegal. Mrs. Friel comes highly recommended by other B&B owners. She serves a home-cooked Irish breakfast, yogurt, fruit, and a choice of cereals. The house has bay windows in front for ocean views and a new conservatory dining room, overlooking ocean, golf courses, lakes, and islands such as Kilclooney Dolmen and Doonfort Ringfort. A beautiful garden graces the front yard with folding chairs to lounge in during the off hours. The rooms are well decorated and furnished and there is a comfortable lounge with a television. You will receive an especially warm welcome, of tea or coffee and baby-sitting can be arranged while you play golf at the nearby 18-hole course or go out for a pint at the local pub. This quiet location has forest and cliff walks and trips to historic monuments and a wild-bird reserve. Visit gorgeous Gweebara Bay, with a long stretch of sandy beaches, just a 10-minute walk away. The water is safe for bathing.

Hilltop House
Judy McDermott
Letterkenny Road
Stranorlar, County Donegal
Telephone: 074-31185
E-mail: admiran@unison.ie
Bedrooms: 3 with private baths
Rates: €25.50-38.50; 25 percent discount for children. Accepts vouchers. **Credit cards:** Yes. **Open:** April 1 to September 30. **Children:** Yes. **Pets:** No. **Smoking:** No. **Provisions for handicapped:** None. **Directions:** Please call owner.

This pretty cottage is in a beautiful setting among the rolling hills of Donegal on the outskirts of the towns of Ballybofey and Stranorlar, known as the twin towns. You'll find three neat, nicely decorated rooms with color-coordinated bed linens, curtains, and lampshades in pleasant pastels. All have bathrooms en suite and each room has television and tea/coffee makers. Breakfast in their conservatory dining room with lovely views makes for a great start to the day. Their varied menu includes Irish smoked salmon with scrambled eggs and home-baked bread. Visitors will be assured of a warm welcome by Judy and all the comforts of a modern home when they visit Hilltop. They are ideally situated for touring Donegal and northern Ireland. You'll find good golfing and fishing nearby. A small boat is available for lake fishing.

ALSO RECOMMENDED

Bruckless, *Bruckless House,* Clive and Joan Evans. Telephone: 073-37071; Fax: 073-37070. Bedrooms: 5, 3 with private baths. Clive breeds traditional Irish draft horses and Connemara ponies. Home handsomely decorated and appointed. On N56 toward Killybegs. Bruckless House is on left in the village of Bruckless.

Killybegs, *Glenlee House,* Mrs. Ellen O'Keeney, Fintra Road. Telephone: 073-31026. Bedrooms: 5, all with private baths. Very nice. Recommended by Mary McGinty of Lough Eske, Donegal.

Killybegs, *Lough Head House,* Mrs. Sadie McKeever, Donegal Road. Telephone: 073-31088. Bedrooms: 3, 2 with private baths. Vouchers accepted. Panoramic view of Killybegs Harbor. Smoke-free home.

Letterkenny, *Pennsylvania House,* Nuala and Michael Duddy, Curraghleas, Mountain Top. Telephone 074-26808; Fax: 074-28905. Bedrooms: 4, 3 en suite. Exceptionally beautiful home with a warm touch of elegance and hospitality. Panoramic views of hills, valleys, and mountains of Donegal. Offers bedroom telephones, facsimile, and photocopying. Four minutes from Letterkenny.

County Dublin

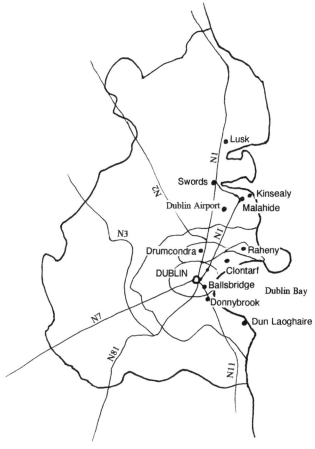

County Dublin is nearly the smallest county in Ireland, but by no means the least important. The capital city of Dublin dominates the area, taking up about one-fifth of the county. Besides the city center, suburban areas such as Clontarf, Drumcondra, Raheny, and Fairview to the north, and Ballsbridge, Donnybrook, Rathmines, and Sandymount to the south, are all considered part of Dublin City.

Dublin Center is a very exciting visit with all its history and culture. The best way to get a sense of it all is to ride a tour bus from O'Connell Street, with colorful commentary, all around, and see the museums, theaters, cathedrals, Trinity College with its famed *Book of Kells,* Saint Stephen's Green, the Liffey River with its "humpy" bridges, well-known Grafton Street (no traffic) for shopping and buskers playing sweet music, the National Gallery and Government buildings, and the Post Office, still with marks of the Easter Rebellion of 1916. For genealogical study, stop at the National Library on Kildare Street and the General Register Office of Births, Marriages, and Deaths at Joyce House, 8/10 Lombard St. East. You may get off at any stop and pick up where you left off in an hour or two and continue the tour.

Dublin City spawned and is very proud of its great writers such as James Joyce, Jonathan Swift, Samuel Beckett, Sean O'Casey, Brendan Behan, Kate O'Brien, Oscar Wilde, Mary Lavin, George Bernard Shaw, Brian Friel, Maeve Binchy, Christy Brown, and many others. Visit the James Joyce Cultural Centre at 35 North Great George's St. There is a whole walking tour you may take of the spots visited by Leopold Bloom, the hero of *Ulysses.* Dublin even celebrates "Bloomsday" on June 16 each year.

Be sure to visit the Dublin Zoo; Phoenix Park; the Bewleys Cafe on Grafton Street, with its delicious fresh coffee and food and its delightful James Joyce Room; and many of the old and charming pubs, some with traditional music. Scan the papers for current plays at the Abbey, the Peacock, and the Gate theaters. We found them very enjoyable. The original Abbey Theater was started by William Yeats and Lady Gregory.

Outlying districts have beautiful old Dublin homes; go east to Howth on a point of land that has the lighthouse called "The Eye of Ireland," and visit the restaurants and the Abbey Tavern in Howth, where a show of traditional Irish music is played nightly. In Clontarf, there is St. Anne's Rose Garden to visit and an excellent restaurant, The Yacht, on Clontarf Road, with super choices and good prices, especially at noon. Of course, Dublin Airport is just 20 minutes from Clontarf, Drumcondra, or Raheny. North and near the airport is the town of Malahide, with its smart castle and grounds and lovely old buildings downtown. To the south Ballsbridge flaunts the R.D.S. Arena with its famous horse shows and other events, and the Jury's Hotel with their nightly cabaret show, which is an extravaganza. Sandymount and Merrion have great beaches. Farther south is Bray Head, a wonderful place to climb, with ocean views., and the lovely seaport of Dún Laoghaire with its beaches and ferries to Holyhead, England. Dún Laoghaire also has the famed Joyce Tower to visit.

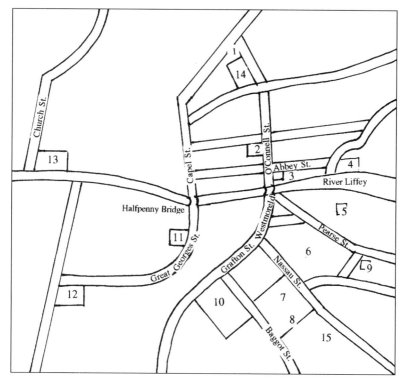

Dublin City

PLACES OF GENERAL PUBLIC INTEREST

1. Writer's Museum	6. Trinity College	11. Dublin Castle
2. General Post Office	7. National Museum	12. St. Patrick's Cathedral
3. Abbey Theatre	8. National Library	13. Four Courts of Justice
4. Central Bus Station	9. Pearse Station	14. Parnell Square
5. Tara St. Station	10. St. Stephen's Green	15. Merrion Square

The DART, a very efficient electrical railway system, operates to outlying areas as far as Howth to the north and Dún Laoghaire to the south. It begins at 6:30 A.M. and ends at 11:30 P.M. There is very extensive bus service to all areas. The Tourist Information Office (Tel. 01-747733) at 14 Upper O'Connell Street is open weekdays 9-5:30 and Saturdays 9-1. The Irish Tourist Board (Tel. 01-765872), at Baggot Street Bridge, is open weekdays only, 9-6.

Ashbrook House
Mrs. Eve Mitchell
River Road
Ashtown, Castleknock
Dublin 15, County Dublin
Telephone and **Fax:** 01-8385660
Bedrooms: 4, all with private baths
Rates: €45 p.p.; single €60. Vouchers not accepted. **Credit cards:** VISA
and MasterCard. **Open:** January 4 to December 20. **Children:** All ages.
Pets: No. **Smoking:** Lounge only. **Provisions for handicapped:** None.
Directions: Take M50 from airport. Exit at N3 turnoff for Blanchard-
town/Castleknock. Turn left at roundabout and onto another round-
about. Go straight until next roundabout with Halfway House Pub
on left. Turn left at pub; go over railway crossing. At next crossroad,
turn left and the house is second gate on left.

This attractive, large, 1897 Georgian home is just 10 minutes from
the airport and ten minutes from Dublin center. The bedrooms are
all very good sized with large baths, and one room has a marble fireplace. Eve has used pinkish salmon, blues, blue and yellow, and pink
and white color schemes in her rooms. Some furniture is pine and
one new room is knotty pine in tea, orange and green color, and
another room is decorated with cranberry and white. All look onto
handsome gardens and countryside views. Eve serves a buffet breakfast of cereals, fruit, juices, besides poached or boiled eggs, bacon,
mushroom, and tomato. There is a grass tennis court on the premises
and golf courses and horse riding areas are available. A good place
to eat is the Halfway House Pub, which is very close by.

Aishling House
Frances and Robert English
19/20 St. Lawrence Road
Clontarf, Dublin 3, County Dublin
Telephone: 01-8339097
Fax: 01-8338400
E-mail: info@aishlinghouse.com
Web: www.aishlinghouse.com
Bedrooms: 9, all with private baths
Rates: €75 p.p. private bath; Single €50 p.p. Vouchers not accepted. 25-50 percent discount for children. Vouchers not accepted. **Credit cards:** VISA and MasterCard. **Open:** All year, except Christmas week. **Children:** All ages. **Pets:** No. **Smoking:** No. **Provisions for handicapped:** None. **Directions:** From Dublin, stay north of the Liffey River, pass bottom of O'Connell Street. Then first left and follow signs for Howth/Malahide. Turn left around Busarus bus station. Go straight up Amiens Street into Fairview, then into Clontarf. Turn left before Yacht Restaurant, onto St. Lawrence Road. Aishling House is on the left.

The Aisling House is two elegant Victorian houses combined and fronted by a lovely rose garden, with a fruit tree orchard and children's area to the rear. The location gives it easy access to the airport, ferry, and city centre. It is beautifully restored with some very large bedrooms to accommodate families. A new cozy sitting room with glass doors is very appealing. All floors are newly polished. Bedrooms vary in style from Victorian floral to fresh, bold colors and luxurious throw quilts on each bed. Each room has a remote-control television. In the dining room, each breakfast table has a different pottery milk jug, preserve bowl, and white and brown sugar bowls. Famous Irish pottery is on display here, and two stunning still-life oil paintings adorn the walls. Frances and Robert want guests to feel at home and relaxed as well. Breakfast consists of homemade compote of fruit, homemade muesli, scones, and breads, all of which compliment a typical cooked Irish breakfast. They offer fruit juice, whole grapefruit segments, and fresh fruits with an assortment of cereals on the side buffet before the main course. New sports complex, with 50 m pool, and golf course are nearby, and many pubs and restaurants are within walking distance.

Torc House
Eileen Kelly
17 Seacourt, St. Gabriels Road
Clontarf, Dublin 3, County Dublin
Telephone: 01-8332547
E-mail: pkellytorc@eircom.net
Bedrooms: 3; 2 with private baths, 1 with shared
Rates: €34 p.p. private bath; €34 p.p. shared bath. Vouchers not accepted. **Credit cards:** None. **Open:** May to October. **Children:** No. **Pets:** No. **Smoking:** No. **Provisions for handicapped:** None. **Directions:** From Dublin, go left on Amiens Street to North Strand and Clontarf Road to Seafield and go left. The first right is St. Gabriels Road, opposite the church.

We have stayed here a number of times and Eileen is a wonderful host, always helpful with a cup of tea at the ready in the comfortable lounge with a television. Her interior-decoration skills show in all her pretty rooms and baths; one room is newly and exotically decorated with red and gold with cream rolled pillows; one has butterscotch flowered duvets with matching print wallpaper; her other is lovely pink, green, and rose. She uses dried bouquets of flowers, and embroidery and lace on her towels. Besides her regular Irish Breakfast, she offers special food for people on low-fat diets, yogurt, fruit and cereal, and sometimes porridge or French toast. The dining room looks out onto a garden terrace and is set with elegant fine china. They can park five cars safely off the street. Eileen has a great grasp of Dublin entertainment and will help with your itinerary. Walk to the beautiful St. Ann's Rose Garden, where there is tennis. You'll be 10 minutes from Howth (with nightly Irish music) and the beach, 20 minutes from the airport, and a walk to a bus for Dublin and all of its great culture and history. We usually book seats for a play when we arrive, as they are numerous and very good in Dublin.

Calderwood House
Mary and Barry Memery
2 Calderwood Road
Drumcondra, Dublin 9, County Dublin
Telephone: 01-8379568
Fax: 01-8379568
E-mail: bmemery@eircom.net
Bedrooms: 5 with private baths
Rates: €33 p.p. private bath. 50 percent discount for children 2-12 years; babies free. Vouchers not accepted. **Credit cards:** VISA and MasterCard. **Open:** Febuary1-November 30. **Children:** All ages. **Pets:** No. **Smoking:** Restricted. **Provisions for handicapped:** None. **Directions:** From the airport, take the N1 to the red-brick church (Whitehall). Go to the fourth set of lights, turn left onto Griffith Avenue, then take your second left. The first two-story building on the right is Calderwood House.

This tall brick building is 15 minutes from the airport or city center. Mary and Barry are very congenial and will help you plan tours through Dublin. Their rooms are decorated in yellows, green, and olives and are all different, neat, and attractive; 3 are on the ground floor and 1 is upstairs. The en-suite one downstairs is all pale pinks and has a garden view. The upstairs room has a high ceiling with a lovely stained-glass window facing west, left over from when the house was a convent. The living and dining rooms have handsome original pine floors. They are proud of their freshly brewed coffee served at the Irish Breakfast with a choice of fruit and yogurt. In the pretty town-house area near Griffith Avenue, the house is close to many colleges and institutions. It is 10 minutes to the city by bus, and beaches, golf, and tennis, and botanic gardens are within 15 minutes' drive.

Annesgrove
Anne D'Alton
28 Rosmeen Gardens
Dún Laoghaire, County Dublin
Telephone: 01-2809801
Bedrooms: 4; 2 with private baths, 2 with shared
Rates: €32 p.p. private bath; €30 p.p. shared bath. 25 percent discount for children under 12. Vouchers not accepted. **Credit cards:** None. **Open:** March 1 to December 15. **Children:** Ages 6 and up. **Pets:** No. **Smoking:** No. **Provisions for handicapped:** None. **Directions:** From town center, take Georges Street south. The first right after the stoplight is Rosmeen Gardens, opposite People's Park. The house is number 28, a few houses up on the left.

This attractive brick and stucco house was built in 1932. Your hostess, Anne D'Alton, exudes a pleasant, professional charm and is always close at hand to look after special requests. The rooms are neat and peaceful, tastefully decorated in greens and beiges with wall trims, duvets, and curtains that match. Mrs. D'Alton has graced her walls with her husband's delicate watercolor landscapes, and they certainly add a lot to the rooms. All rooms have sinks and plenty of heat and hot water. Bathrooms are updated with pretty tiles. The sitting room has a television and is quite cozy. The dining room, where you'll be served an Irish Breakfast and a choice of fruit or yogurt or porridge, cereal, and juice, looks out onto delightfully landscaped gardens a few steps down on a lower level. If you must leave before breakfast, Mrs. D'Alton offers a special rate. They are very close to People's Park, the waterfront and ferry terminal, buses, and the DART into Dublin. Visit the many fine restaurants in town, swim at Sandy Cove Beach, and play golf or tennis very nearby. The D'Altons will tell you where. And the DART ride into Dublin is only 20 minutes. Dún Laoghaire is an ideal location to start or finish a holiday in the Irish Republic.

Windsor Lodge
Mary O'Farrell
3 Islington Avenue
Sandycove, DúnLaoghaire
County Dublin
Telephone and **Fax:** 01-2846952
E-mail: winlodge@eircom.net
Bedrooms: 4 with private baths
Rates: €32-35 p.p. 50 percent discount children under 12. **Credit cards:** No. **Open:** January 1 to December 23. **Children:** All ages. **Pets:** No. **Smoking:** No. **Provisions for handicapped:** None. **Directions:** Drive 1 km from Dún Laoghaire ferry entrance (sea on left). Turn right away from sea at South Bank Restaurant. House is on the left.

This Victorian home is only 30 meters from the sea front with views of Dublin Bay. It is close to town, the shops, the ferry to England, the DART, and buses to Dublin Center. Mary is a helpful hostess, giving hints on places to visit and the best restaurants in her area. Her bedrooms are large, neat, and attractive, with flowered quilts, original watercolors, and lovely prints. All have tea/coffee makers. She serves a full Irish breakfast with sausage and home-baked bread, also offers cereal, yogurt, cheese, and fruit. Take the pier walk on the waterfront; visit James Joyce Tower at Sandycove Point. Eat at the Eagle Pub or Bistro Vino in Sandycove. Tuscana is another very good restaurant. We had lunch at Juggy's Well and were more than satisfied.

Liscara
Jane Kiernan
Malahide Road
Kinsealy, County Dublin
Telephone: 01-8483751
Fax: 01-8483751
Bedrooms: 6, all with private baths
Rates: €32.; Single €45; 25 percent discount for children. Vouchers not accepted. **Credit cards:** None. **Open:** March 1 to October 30. **Children:** Over 5. **Pets:** No. **Smoking:** No. **Provisions for handicapped:** Yes, one ground-floor room can take wheelchair. **Directions:** Drive to Fairview, then turn left on Malahide Road at end of park. Liscara is one mile on right after third roundabout.

This brand-new, red-brick manor house is a treat. On one acre, there are cabbage fields and a nursery to the back of it. Jane Kiernan is very attentive. Her husband is newly retired. The rooms are all large and elegant; one is dark lavender, white, and pink; one double has a spectacular view of fields and way out to the water and Howth. Another room is robin's-egg blue. There is a room on the first floor with wide bathroom access for the handicapped. The handsome dining room has three tables, a flowered white wall, and a teal rug. In addition to her standard full Irish breakfast, Jane serves fresh fruit and yogurt and cheese or kippered herrings. There is baby-sitting available here by their daughter. They are close to golf courses in Malahide and Portmarnock, and fishing, boating, and bowling are also easily accessible. There is a Cinema 10 nearby and they are only 6 minutes to the airport. Charming Malahide town and castle are two minutes away. The N50 motorway is one mile away.

Pebble Mill B&B
Monica Fitzsimons
Off Malahide Road
Kinsealy, County Dublin
Telephone and **Fax:** 01-8461792
Bedrooms: 3, all with private baths
Rates: €35-45 p.p. 50 percent discount for children. Vouchers not accepted. **Credit cards:** MasterCard. **Open:** January to November. **Children:** 4 and up. **Pets:** No. **Smoking:** Lounge only. **Provisions for handicapped:** None. **Directions:** From the airport, take the N1 to the first roundabout, go all around, head back, and take the first left at Coachman's Inn. Go over a humpy bridge drive approximately ³/₄ km, and take the first left marked Kinsealy. Drive for 1 km and at T-junction go right onto Malahide Road; watch for the sign on the right for Pebble Mill. Turn left opposite the sign. The house is on the left.

This stately neo-Georgian house sits on 4 acres in a farm area. The long driveway winds up with flower baskets hanging from posts on either side. The family ponies are in a corral next to the house. The decor in the large living room with television is modern and creative. It has a white marble fireplace, very comfortable chairs, a carved horse, and a green rug. Monica, very kind and personable, puts you at ease from the start. All the rooms are large, attractive, painted cream, and have cream bedspreads. They have big windows, views of gardens, televisions, and hair dryers. The dining room is red and white with a sliding glass door to the outside. Along with her full Irish breakfast you may have fruit or yogurt. The beach is 5 minutes away, and horse-back riding, tennis, and golf are 10 minutes away, as well as Malahide Castle and town. It is only 6 minutes from the airport.

ALSO RECOMMENDED

Donnybrook, *Hazelhurst,* Joan Donnellan, 166 Stillorgan Road. Telephone: 01-2838509. Bedrooms: 6, with private baths. Modern townhouse right on the N11, across from University College Dublin. Extra-large living room with fireplace for reading and writing. Major credit cards accepted. Accessible to City Center and Dún Laoghaire ferry.

Dún Laoghaire, *Duncree,* Mrs. C. O'Sullivan, 16 Northumberland. Telephone: 01-2806118. Bedrooms: 4, all shared bath but with sink and mirror in rooms. Modest home but very nice hostess. Within walking distance of shops and restaurants.

Sutton, *Dun Aoibhinn,* Mary McDonnell, 30 Sutton Park, Dublin 13 (North County). Telephone and Fax: 01-9325456. Bedrooms: 3, all en suite. Luxurious detached home in quiet residential area. Adjacent coast road. Five-minute walk to bus and DART. Recommended by John and Sue Ley, Harrowgate, Yorkshire, UK.

County Galway

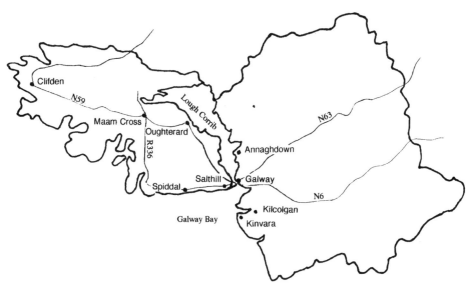

County Galway is one of the largest counties in Ireland and Galway City is known as the capital of the west of Ireland. This county has a ruggedness of terrain that differs from the soft greens of the south. Galway, with its rivers, mountains, bays, lakes, and seacoast, is very photogenic. In north Galway, have a look at the peaceful Killary Harbor, which separates Mayo and Galway. The fields of green sweeping down to blue water and gentle hills beyond are a sight to behold. Between tiny Leenane on the border and Letterfrack, visit the Kylemore Abbey. Although Letterfrack seems to be in the boondocks, there is a lovely woolen craft shop there with a tearoom with sandwiches and scones. Stay along the N59 to reach the stunning town of Clifden, called the capital of Connemara, sitting high on a hill. It has marvelous views of bays and high mountains, such as the Twelve Bens, which change colors with the light and the season.

Clifden has joys of its own—pretty B&Bs with views, excellent restaurants, and traditional Irish music right into October. We tried

Mitchell's Restaurant and D'Arcy Inn; both were quite good. It's fun to shop and browse through the art galleries, too. When you tear yourself away from the specialness of Clifden, drive around along the coast and visit the pretty fishing towns of Roundstone and Cashel. For a shorter drive, go down the N59 through rough and rocky Connemara country (look for ponies and donkeys grazing) to Oughterard. This pretty town is right on Lake Corrib, which reportedly has the best fishing in Ireland.

Salthill and Galway town are tied together and are noted for their beaches, called strands, and boardwalks. Salthill has the very large Leisureland Amusement Park, with a swimming pool and rides, and an 18-hole golf course. It's a refreshing walk along the beach just outside of Galway. Look for the Galway hookers, special fishing boats with very rounded sides and sails.

Galway City is old, with one-way streets and many, many shops and eating places. There are art galleries and two theaters, the An Tarbhdhearc on Middle Street and the Druid on Chapel Lane. Catch an Irish music session any evening in summer at one of the many pubs. At the end of July or the beginning of August, the famous Galway Races run for 6 days with much music and festivities. Book way ahead, for the Irish fill the rooms for this event. Another event you might enjoy is the Oyster Festival the third or fourth weekend in September.

We spent some time in Spiddal, west of Galway, where a lot of Gaelic is spoken in the pubs, the accents are strong and melodious, and the spontaneous fiddling and singing is good. From Galway City, the N6 takes you straight across the mid-section of the country to Dublin. Visit the starkly beautiful Aran Islands at the opening of Galway Bay. It's a happy trip back in time.

South of Galway you'll find the sweet town of Kilcolgan, with its fishing rivers, and a bit farther there is the important, pretty, small town of Kinvara. This town has farms and horseback riding, Dunguaire Castle with a feast and costumes, and a little port with pastel buildings looking out on fishing boats sitting at the docks. We couldn't resist painting some of these scenes. Eat at Partners Restaurant: good food, good prices.

From Galway City, the N6 takes you straight across the midsection of the country to the N4 and on to Dublin. The town of Athenry, just to the east of Galway City, is noted in the song, "Fields of Athenry," an Irish favorite. Visit the castle there. In October, the largest Horse and Cattle Fair in Europe is held farther on at Ballinasloe out on the eastern border of the county.

Corrib View Farm
Mary Scott-Furey
Annaghdown, County Galway
Telephone: 091-791114
E-mail: mscottfurey@hotmail.com
Bedrooms: 4; 3 with private bath; 1 with shared bath
Rates: €34 p.p. with private bath; €32 p.p. for shared bath. **Credit
cards:** None. **Open:** April to October. **Children:** Yes, 4 years and up.
Pets: no. **Smoking:** No. **Provisions for handicapped:** None. **Directions:** 10 minutes north of Galway city. 3 km off Galway-Headford-
Castlebar Road (N84 road). Sign posted at Cloonboo Cross near
Regan's Bar-Restaurant.

This award-winning, one-hundred-year-old family-farm bed and
breakfast, surrounded by pretty lawns and wonderful landscaped gardens, is located in a scenic setting alongside Lough Corrib. It has a
bright and airy dining room in soft pink with matching tablecloths
and china at each separate table. The sitting room is tastefully decorated in peach and brown, with a nearby writing area. All the bedrooms are in varying shades of orchid and white. Tea/coffee-making
facilities are in bedrooms. Homemade breads and jams and home-
grown fruit are included in their delicious full Irish farm breakfast.
The location midway between Galway and Headford is ideal for touring Connemara. Mary with vast knowledge of the region will help
you plan day trips to Connemara and the Aran Islands, or locally, trips
to Annaghdown Pier and Abbey ruins, or hiring a boat on Lough Corrib. There is also a horse riding center nearby. The less adventurous
can relax in the leisure garden at the farm. Visit St. Brendan's
Monastery ruins.

Beach View House
Bridie Conneely
Oatquarter, Kilronan
Aran Islands (Inis Mór), County Galway
Telephone and **Fax:** 099-61141
E-mail: beachviewhouse@eircom.net
Bedrooms: 6, 3 with private baths
Rates: €26 p.p.; €38 single; 25 percent discount for children under 12.
Vouchers accepted. **Credit cards:** None. **Open:** May1 to September
30. **Children:** All ages. **Pets:** Yes. **Smoking:** Only in lounge. **Provisions
for handicapped:** None. **Directions:** Take a ferry to Inis Mór from Gal-
way or Rossaveal; the bus to Rossaveal is provided with the ferry ticket.
From the port on the island, take a bus, pony trap, bike, or walk 6
km to the B&B.

Beach View is a large, family-run home with a sitting area in the
front yard. It is situated in a tranquil spot in the center of the island.
Bridie Conneely is charming and friendly. The 6 bedrooms are neat
and delightfully furnished in pleasing colors. Bridie includes scones
with her full Irish breakfast. Recreational features in the area are
horseback riding, fishing, cycling, and swimming just two miles away
on the safe, sandy beach. The house is within walking distance to
famous Fort Dun Aengus and convenient to a restaurant and pub. Inis
Mor, "The Big Island," has the only harbor suitable for steamer dock-
ing. You may take a jaunting car ride around the island to see ring
forts or Dun Aengus perched on a 300-foot cliff above the sea. Bikes
are for rent, too. You may take ferries to other fascinating unique
Aran Islands during your stay. Gaelic is the everyday language, but
polite islanders will speak English.

Pier House
Maura Joyce
Lower Kilronan, Inish Mór
Aran Islands, County Galway
Telephone: 099-61417
Fax: 099-61122
E-mail: pierh@iol.ie
Bedrooms: 12, all with private baths
Rates: €45-60. **Credit cards:** visa and MasterCard. **Open:** March to
November. **Children:** Yes. **Pets:** Yes. **Smoking:** Limited. **Provisions for
handicapped:** Some. **Directions:** From the ferry from Rossaveal, walk
directly up the dock and you are facing Pier House across the street.

   This attractive, large, welcoming three-star inn sits upon a small hill
and many of the rooms have an ocean view. In the building, there is
also a wonderful restaurant with unique items for all three meals.
Breakfast with fresh scones is served in the restaurant for the price of
the room. The inn has a large lounge with couches, tables, a television, a long porch with umbrella tables for lunches or snacks, and
seats for sunning. The rooms are all large with televisions, telephones,
hair dryers, and tea/coffee makers. There is well-placed lighting for
reading. All rooms are carpeted and have flowered or checked bedspreads in rich colors of greens, blues, and reds. Pier House is within
walking distance of many of the lively pubs and shops. Take the little
bus tour of the island or a pony-trap ride for just ten euros. A visit to
Dun Aengus Ring Fort is a must! The restaurant within serves many
creative dishes, such as large prawns or sesame-encrusted salmon fish
cakes with Tai lime sauce.

Seacrest B&B
Geraldine Faherty
Kilronan, Inish Mór
Aran Islands, County Galway
Telephone: 099-61292
Fax: 099-61429
Bedrooms: 6, all with private baths
Rates: €25-28. Discount for children. **Credit cards:** MasterCard and VISA. **Open:** January 10 to December 1. **Children:** All ages. **Pets:** No. **Smoking:** Dining room only. **Provisions for handicapped:** None. **Directions:** Follow the main road past Pier House and on along the sea. Seacrest is a few houses in from the corner, on the right just past the Fisherman's Restaurant.

This modern stucco house is painted yellow with orange trim. It is a homey place, just a short walk from the ferry landing. Geraldine will give you a warm welcome of tea or coffee. She lived for a time in Rhode Island, but she says her kids love living on Inish Mór. It certainly is a fascinating place to visit. You step back in time when you walk around early in the morning and see the chickens clucking outside the bright yellow Lucky Star Bar, waiting for the owner to feed them. Pony traps are clopping back and forth, taking people on rides around the island. The Fahertys serve an Irish "Fry," or anything else you might like, such as cereal, fruit, yogurt, and homemade breads. From the bright, large dining room, you might get a peek at the sea. The rooms are attractive, with matching quilts and drapes in colors of green, pale terracotta, or blue and yellow. The roomy bathrooms are nicely tiled. There is a small lounge at the end of the dining room for television watching. You must visit the dramatic Ring Fort way up on the cliffs, called Dun Aengus.

Faul House
Kathleen Conneely
Faul, Clifden, Ballyconneely Road
County Galway
Telephone: 095-21239
Fax: 095-21998
E-mail: info@faulhouse.com
Bedrooms: 6, all with private baths
Rates: €32-35 p.p. 10 percent discount for children. Vouchers accepted. **Credit cards**: No. **Open:** March15 to November 1. **Provisions for handicapped:** None. **Directions:** From Clifden, go 1 mile on Ballyconneely Road to Connemara Pottery. Turn right at pottery sign, then go 1 mile on a narrow winding road. The farmhouse is sign posted.

This lovely modern farmhouse in the Connemara area has large rooms upstairs with farm and water views. The rooms downstairs are smaller and all are handsomely decorated in soft pastels and have hair dryers and tea/coffee makers. Some are family rooms. Michael breeds Connemara ponies for show, and with Brownie, the dog, they keep the flock of mountain sheep in shape. They tend their own hens and ducks on the 35 acres of land. Their lounge has a fireplace with peat burning and there is a small television lounge. Your breakfast will be of many choices, like smoked salmon, cheeses, fruit, yogurts, fresh farm eggs, homemade brown bread, and full Irish. It is served in a lovely dining room with gorgeous views. This is a place for peace and quiet. There are many nice hikes to take to the sea and around the farm. Riding, golfing, fishing, boating, and mountain climbing are all in the area. AA lists the B&B with 4 *Q*s.

Mallmore Country House
Kathleen Hardman
Ballyconneely Road
Clifden, County Galway
Telephone: 095-21460
E-mail: mallmore@indigo.ie
Bedrooms: 6, all with private baths, plus separate full bath with tub
Rates: €30 p.p.; 20 percent discount for children. Vouchers not accepted. **Credit cards:** None. **Open:** March 15 to October 1. **Children:** All ages. **Pets:** No. **Smoking:** Restricted. **Provisions for handicapped:** 4 steps in front but, after that, all on 1 floor. **Directions:** Outside Clifden 1 mile on Ballyconneely Road, look for Mallmore House sign on the right. Turn right at Connemara Pottery. Go up a narrow country road to their gate.

This is a beautiful 1789 Georgian manor house that was built on Clifden Bay by a John D'Arcy, founder of Clifden. It reminds you of a French country home because of its rich flocked walls, arched doorways, and pretty hall lights. It has been completely renovated by the Hardmans. The dining room is luxurious with red wall paper, antique vases and side tables, 6 to 8 separate meal tables covered with linens, ballooned curtains at all windows with shutters, and a fireplace Award winning breakfasts include, pancakes, omellettes, and smoked salmon. The spacious bedrooms are also handsomely decorated with armoires and velvet boudoir chairs, and some have bowed windows viewing the cheery garden and the scenic harbor beyond. Our room was a suite, with two antique chairs in the bowed window where we enjoyed reading and even watercolor painting. Rooms are decorated in soft pastels. The sitting room with a fire is ideal for curling up with a good book. The Hardmans take special care of their guests and run the inn with a steady, gentle touch. Beach, golfing, cycling, fishing, and pony rides nearby.

Winnowing Hill
Margaret Kelly
Ballyconneely Road
Clifden, County Galway
Telephone and **Fax:** 095-21281
E-mail: winnowinghill@eircom.net
Bedrooms: 4, with private baths
Rates: €24-26. 33.3 percent discount for children. **Credit cards:** None.
Open: March 15 to November 5. **Children:** Yes. **Pets:** No. **Smoking:** No.
Provisions for handicapped: None. **Directions:** From Clifden, go1 mile
on Ballyconneely Road to Connemara Pottery and Mallmore House. At
this sign, turn right and head up steep hill to the left to the B&B.

This alpine-like cottage is situated on a tranquil hill overlooking
the Twelve Bens (mountains), Clifden town, and Salt Lake. The views
from the glass conservatory, where Margaret offers you a cup of tea,
are breathtakingly beautiful. I stayed there with my sister, Carol, and
we both loved sitting out there watching clouds change and roll by.
Mrs. Kelly is a terrific hostess, being very informative about points of
interest and musical events in town. Even in May, there are pubs
where Irish music is played. We enjoyed the offerings of fruit and
muesli, oatmeal, and an Irish fry, which includes eggs and sausage or
a Canadian-like bacon. Our large room upstairs was painted in the
prettiest lavender with matching sheets, flowered duvets, and water-
color paintings on the walls. Other rooms were equally attractive. I
photographed a view of the mountains through her glass conservat-
tory windows and a stand of huge calla lilies that Margaret said had
been blooming for months. There is a very homey, welcoming feeling
at this house and you are close to town, fishing, horseback riding,
golfing, and some wonderful hikes.

High Tide
Pat Greaney
9 Grattan Park
Galway City, County Galway
Telephone and **Fax:** 091-584324
E-mail: hightide@iol.ie
Bedrooms: 4, all with private baths
Rates: €27-29 p.p. 20 percent discount for children. Vouchers accepted. **Credit cards:** VISA and MasterCard. **Open:** February 1 to December 1. **Children:** All ages. **Pets:** No. **Smoking:** No. **Provisions for handicapped:** Yes. **Directions:** Take the coast road from city center toward Salthill. The house is midway between the two.

High Tide is a modern two-story home overlooking Galway Bay, with panoramic views of the ocean and Clare Hill. A small flower garden graces its front. The bedrooms are well decorated in soft pastel shades with all conveniences. Some have superb views of the bay. Pat will serve you a wonderful Irish breakfast or other choices of eggs, cereals and fruits. This B&B is close to the fishing village of Claddagh, home of the world famous Claddagh Betrothal Ring. It is a 10 minute walk from the city of Tribes (Galway). The old Anglo-Norman town sits side by side with the new University city. Galway, a young vibrant city, boasts excellent theaters and music. It is the gateway to the Connemara and the Aran Islands. Pat will arrange tours on bus rides to these areas. There is swimming, golf, horseback riding, and tennis in the area.

Moytura
Rita Conway
Ballybane Road
Ballybane, Galway, County Galway
Telephone: 091-757755
E-mail: moyturarc@eircom.net
Web: www.moyturagalway.com
Bedrooms: 4, with private baths
Rates: €30-45; 25 percent discount for children (free up to age 4).
Accepts vouchers. **Credit cards:** VISA and MasterCard. **Open:** January
1 to December 31. **Children:** All ages. **Pets:** No. **Smoking:** No. **Provisions for handicapped:** Ground-floor rooms. **Directions:** Take Route
338 off the N6 to Galway City east, having passed through Oranmore
Village. The B&B is beside the Corrib Great Southern Hotel.

This newly decorated townhouse was the highlight of one Californian's recent two-week vacation in Ireland. She speaks of the delicious
breakfasts and the generosity of Rita with her time—helping to plan
sightseeing trips, even dropping her off downtown twice. The rooms
are lovely and comfortable with luxurious linens on the beds. Upstairs
rooms have a view of the famed Burren and some have a view of Galway Bay. There is a guest television lounge and private car parking.
On your arrival, Rita will greet you with a tea tray. Her breakfasts
include full Irish, home baking, a variety of cereals, juices, grapefruit
segments, prunes, and special diet requests will be honored. From
here you may go swimming, fishing, cycling, horseback riding, golfing, and hear traditional Irish music in pubs. It's a short drive to Connemara National Park, Kylemore Abbey, and the ferry to the Aran
Islands. Rita recommends restaurants "comparable to San Francisco's
best." The visitor also recommends that you stay two nights, as we do.

Clareview House
Brenda McTigue
Kinvara, County Galway
Telephone: 091-637170
Fax: 091-637755
E-mail: clareviewhouse@eircom.net
Bedrooms: 5, all with private baths
Rates: € 30 p.p.; Single €5 extra; 25 percent discount for children.
Vouchers accepted. € 20 dinner. **Credit cards:** None. **Open:** March 1
to November 1. **Children:** All ages. **Pets:** Small. **Smoking:** No. **Provisions for handicapped:** None. **Directions:** From the town of Kinvara,
go north to Dunguaire Castle, then take the road on right, and go 3
km. The farm is on the left.

This 1890, two-story, country-cream farmhouse is set back behind
gates on lovely grounds with flower gardens. It is a 120-acre dairy and
beef farm. Brenda and her shepherd will greet you and offer you a
relaxing tea by the fire in the black marble fireplace. The lounge has
a special antique buffet. The rooms are very neat and pretty, done in
green and peach, pale green and cream, and off-white. All the bathrooms are large. All rooms have a great view of the countryside and
garden. Brenda's full Irish breakfast includes black and white pudding,
fresh scones, cheeses, and fruit. You may have dinner of salmon, trout,
or lamb roast. Relax after dinner in the large new conservatory. Since
the farm is centrally located, you may go 3 km to the charming town of
Kinvara, with its nature walks, shops, colored buildings, nice little
restaurants, and fishing boats in the harbor; or to the Dunguaire Castle, where there is medieval banquet and show, all reserved. There is
a 18-hole golf course in Gort; Coole Park with wildlife in Gort; the Burren and Ailwee Caves just south of Kinvara; boat trips, fishing, and
swimming at Traught Beach just north; and you'll be only 15 miles
from Galway City and 30 miles to Lahinch and Cliffs of Moher.

Roncalli House
Tim and Carmel O'Halloran
24 Whitestrand Avenue
Lower Salthill, County Galway
Telephone and **Fax:** 091-584159
E-mail: roncallihouse@eircon.net
Bedrooms: 6, all with private baths
Rates: 30 p.p.; 20 percent discount for children. Vouchers accepted.
Credit Cards: VISA and MasterCard. **Open:** All year. **Children:** Yes.
Pets: No. **Smoking:** No. **Provisions for handicapped:** None. **Directions:** From Tourist Office, follow signs for Salthill, over Wolfe Tone Bridge, through 3 lights on to Y junction. Turn left. The house on the right, on the corner of 336.

The O'Hallorans have a lovely modern and comfortable two-story home beside Galway Bay, within walking distance of the city center. Warm Irish hospitality greets you as you have your welcoming tea by the fireplace. There are two ground-floor bedrooms and four others upstairs, all done in soft pastel colors with sinks and built-in wardrobes. All have television, hair dryers, and tea/coffee facilities. There is a sunny front lounge and two outdoor patios for guest use. There is central heating and good parking in front. Carmel is proud of the fact that Chelsea Clinton, the president's daughter, stayed here with her entourage for two nights.

Nearby there is a large swimming complex, golf, tennis and horse riding. Salthill is a popular Irish tourist spot. Many excellent restaurants/pubs are available locally, in town or on the road going out to Spiddal. You may walk to city center.

Ard Mhuire
Pat and Teresa McDonagh
Knocknacarra Road
Salthill, County Galway
Telephone: 091-522344
Fax: 091-529629
E-mail: ard@ardmhuire.com
Bedrooms: 6, all with private baths, plus separate full bath
Rates: €40 p.p.; Single €30; 25 percent discount for children under 12. Vouchers accepted. **Credit cards:** MasterCard and VISA. **Open:** January 1 to December 20. **Children:** Yes. **Pets:** No. **Smoking:** No. **Provisions for handicapped:** Yes. **Directions:** Go out along the water from city center, along Promenade, where Leisureland is located on your right, toward Barna. When you get to Spinnaker House Hotel on the left, the next right is Knocknacarra Road. Ard Mhuire is in the second block on the left, a white home with Spanish arches in front and a white wall.

This charming modern home has a nice ambience. Rooms are spacious and nicely decorated. Floral grey and white, pale apricot and green, and pink rose are used in an elegant manner. You don't feel crowded in this home as in some B&Bs. The tiled baths are extra large in 4 of the rooms; some have tubs and showers. All combinations of beds are available, from twins to doubles to triples, so if you reserve early you should get the right accommodations. The gorgeous honeymoon suite with a view of the sea has a king-sized bed with an inset classic archway above, a bright floral-print bedcover, and blue-green walls—very nice! The breakfast menu is a full Irish breakfast served at a large antique, hand-carved table and chairs or at separate small side tables. A lovely small conservatory was added in 1998. The large lounge adjoins the dining area. Mrs. McDonagh is a pleasant hostess who makes you feel right at home and whom we enjoyed chatting with over tea and homemade scones.

Carraig Beag
Catherine Lydon
1 Burren View Heights
Salthill, County Galway
Telephone: 091-521696
Bedrooms: 5, all with private baths
Rates: €30-36 p.p. ⅓ discount for children. Vouchers not accepted.
Credit cards: None. **Open:** All year, except Christmas week. **Children:**
Yes. **Pets:** No. **Smoking:** Restricted. **Provisions for handicapped:** 1
room, on first floor. **Directions:** Pass the golf course, take the second
road on the right across from Spinnaker. The Cottage Shop is at the
corner. Go up Knocknacarra to the second B&B on the left.

Pretty flowers adorn the front of this modern brick home, with its
look of a stately manor house. It is even more attractive inside with
its handsome wood doors, broad staircase, and elegant large dining
room with crystal chandelier, adjoining a large living room with marble fireplace for relaxing. Guests have a cozy separate lounge with a
television. The spacious rooms are handsomely decorated in pinks
and whites, green and greys, and wine colors, all with tea/coffee facilities and television. Some have views. Breakfast is served on a large
lace-covered table where you can even view the water through the
living room. There are separate tables also. Breakfast is a full Irish
cooked one with home-baked goods and fruit. Catherine Lydon is
gracious and dignified yet a charming and friendly hostess who will
make your stay in Galway a pleasant and memorable one. She will be
quite willing to guide you to the best places for walks, golfing, horseback riding, fishing, or short trips, such as to the Aran Islands, Connemara, or the Burren. She will even tell you about the special sights
and traditional music in Galway.

The Connaught
Colette and Tom Keaveney
Barna Road
Salthill, County Galway
Telephone and **Fax:** 091-525865
E-mail: tcconnaught@eircom.net
Bedrooms: 6; 5 with private baths, 1 with shared
Rates: €26 p.p. private bath; €24 shared bath. Vouchers accepted.
Credit cards: None. **Open:** March 16 to November 15. **Children:** All
ages. **Pets:** No. **Smoking:** No. **Provisions for handicapped:** None.
Directions: Drive west along the water from Galway town and con-
tinue on Salthill until you pass the golf club. Come to a T-junction and
turn left at Knocknacarra Cross onto Barna Road. The Connaught is
600 yards on the right.

This is a bright and cheerful Georgian home, probably made so
by the Keaveneys. It has a salmon pink exterior and handsome interior. Good-sized bedrooms, all on the second floor, are redone in
soft pastel colors and are furnished with twin or double beds (some
triples), electric blankets, and nice mirrors. There is access to a large
balcony facing Rusheen Bay from two of the rooms. This is nice for
lounging in the sun. Downstairs is a cozy, pink and brown guest
lounge with a television and stone fireplace. Breakfast is a full Irish
cooked one with homemade brown bread and possibly some other
pastries, fruit on the buffet, and fresh brewed coffee, served at separate tables. Tom teaches baking and confectionary at a local college,
so he provides some added treats to the menu such as his famous
croissants. After this hearty breakfast, you can play golf at a nearby
championship 18-hole course or go for some water fun at the indoor
pool down the road at Leisureland. This young couple is very likeable.

Marian Lodge
Mrs. Celine Molloy
Knocknacarra Road
Salthill, County Galway
Telephone: 091-521678
Fax: 091-528103
E-mail: celine@iol.ie
Web: www.marian-lodge.com
Bedrooms: 6, all with private baths
Rates: €30-40 p.p. ⅓ discount for children. Vouchers accepted. **Credit cards:** MasterCard and VISA. **Open:** All year except Christmas. **Children:** Yes. **Pets:** No. **Smoking:** No. **Provisions for handicapped:** None.
Directions: Go along the water from Galway to Salthill; pass Leisureland on the right. Across from Spinnaker turn right on Knocknacarra Road. The home is on the left, with a sign above the wall to the right of the driveway.

The smell of fresh-baked goods greets you as you enter Marian Lodge. You will receive an especially warm welcome from Celine when you arrive. She and her husband, Pat, are very friendly and most anxious to please. This is a cozy and restful place with lots of good food and comfortable rooms with orthopedic beds, televisions, tea/coffee-making facilities, telephones, and clock radios. Rooms are decorated in blues, greens, and pinks, with reading lights over the beds and many combinations of beds to suit the traveling public. There is a trouser press on the landing. Some rooms have showers and large tubs in the bathrooms. The living room or lounge has a television and a brick fireplace with old antique pots and a barrel of peat for burning. Celine tells how her house was built quite recently with solid concrete walls so as to keep it quiet inside. Breakfast is the traditional Irish one and includes fresh-baked scones and soda bread. They have tickets here for deep-sea fishing and windsurfing. They are close to a 22-hole golf course, swimming at Leisureland, horseback riding, and a bus to the Aran Islands. They have private car parking.

Marless House
Mary Geraghty
Threadneedle Road
Salthill, County Galway
Telephone: 091-523931
Fax: 091-529810
E-mail: marlesshouse@eircom.net
Web: www.marlesshouse.com
Bedrooms: 6, all with private baths
Rates: €29-32 p.p. 25 percent discount for children under 12. Vouchers accepted. **Credit cards:** VISA and MasterCard. **Open:** All year.
Children: Yes. **Pets:** No. **Smoking:** No. **Provisions for handicapped:** None. **Directions:** Take the street along the water from Galway town, past Leisureland. About 2 km from Galway, turn right on Threadneedle Road. The B&B is on the right, a pretty, Georgian, two-story with a brick front, white pedimented entrance, and white sides.

This beautiful modern Georgian brick home is spacious and decorated with fine woodwork and bright colors. Mary is a generous and kind hostess and spends a lot of time with guests. Her attention to details and good management results in a pleasant stay. She jokes that her husband, Tom, who cooks on weekends, is her "honeydew" husband: "Honey, do this, and honey, do that." We were impressed with the comfort, size, and decor of our bedroom and bathroom. Our room was a bright cheery yellow and white. You can have your breakfast on the large dining-room table, if you like to chat with fellow travelers, or at separate tables, if you want privacy. The juice, fruit, cereal, and yogurt are self-service on the side buffet. Delicious hot entrées and beverage orders are brought to your table. The living room is warmly decorated in apricot and blue-green with a white fireplace. Mary encourages guests to walk the Promenade along the beautiful Galway Bay or indulge in the many recreational activities, such as golf, swimming, tennis, and horseback riding. Beach just 100 yards away.

Ardmor Country House
Vera Feeney
Greenhill
Spiddal, County Galway
Telephone: 091-553145
Fax: 091-553596
E-mail: ardmor@ireland.com
Bedrooms: 7, all with private baths
Rates: €30 p.p. Vouchers accepted. **Credit cards:** No. **Open:** March through December. **Children:** All ages. **Pets:** No. **Smoking:** No. **Provisions for handicapped:** Yes, in *Guide to Handicapped.* **Directions:** Go out to Spiddal from Galway, through Barna on R336. It is 8 miles to Spiddal (10 miles from city center). The house is ½ mile west of Spiddal town on the left.

This lovely modern home, surrounded by a beautifully landscaped garden, boasts a panoramic view of the bay and the Burren beyond. Vera Feeney is a very well organized, experienced, and gracious hostess. Mr. Feeney is related to the John Ford family of the film *The Quiet Man.* Mrs. Feeney will even arrange a trip to the Aran Islands from Rossaveal. The blue or pink bedrooms are very trim and comfortable. Each has 2 or 3 beds with a vanity and sink in separate alcoves, in addition to a private, tiled bathroom. We enjoyed the huge dining/living room with a fireplace for Vera's award-winning breakfasts, and the delightful chats with other guests on the comfy sofas. Rollicking traditional music can be heard in Spiddal at Hughes Pub almost every night. Plenty of good restaurants in Spiddal are budget priced and very good meals are available in the Bridge House Hotel. We enjoyed the *Bolvisce* restaurant for its coziness and great seafood. Activities available here are fishing, riding, golf, watersports, and swimming at safe sandy beaches within walking distance, and bus tours to Connemara. Enjoy drinks and tea on large balcony overlooking the sea and award-winning gardens.

ALSO RECOMMENDED

Aran Islands, *Cois Cuain,* Martin Faherty, Innis Meain, 100 yards from pier. Telephone: 099-73097, Sister Brid: 01-8382132. Sleeps 20. Bed-and-breakfast or self-catering accomodations all year.

Clifden, *Failte B&B,* Maureen Kelly, Ardbear. Telephone: 095-21159. Bedrooms: 5, 2 en suite. 2 km from town, off Ballyconneely Road.

Oughterard, *Corrib Wave House,* Maria and Michael Healy, Connemara (located 2 miles east of Oughterard off the N59). Telephone: 091-552147. **Fax:** 091-552736 Bedrooms: 8, 6 with private baths. Lakeside farmhouse with panoramic view. Boats, engines, and boatmen available for hire.

County Kerry

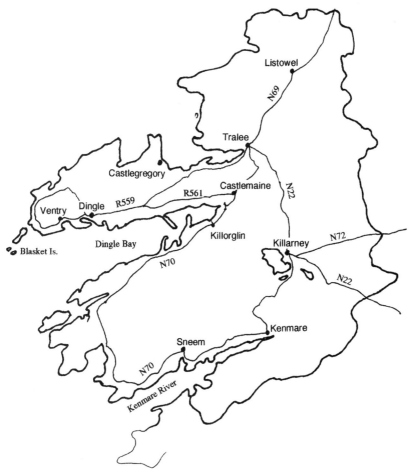

County Kerry is a wonderful blend of purple mountains, green pastures, sea cliffs, smooth beaches, old castles, ancient ruins, and history. Dingle, our favorite town in Ireland, still retains the flavor of a small traditional town in spite of all the tourists who flock there in summer. You'll hear Gaelic spoken in shops and pubs and all street signs are in both Gaelic and English. Gaelic sounds like Danish or Norwegian.

The beauty and serenity of blue Dingle Bay dominates the town. It is still a fishing village, so you may go to the docks of Dingle and watch them unload fish. In summer, you'll note young folks rowing or racing black curraghs (boats made of treated skins). The Slieve Mish Mountains in the background are impressive. Buildings all a different color, stairstepping up the hilly main street, make a beguiling scene.

We found some good sales in the shops, and we were satisfied each time we visited The Forge Restaurant. A favorite lunch place is An Cafe Litearta, a bookstore with a café in the rear that serves everything including decaf coffee, great soups, and hot scones. O'Flaherty's Pub is where you go for music. Some summer nights the walls bend in and out with the rollicking crowds. Try the beach in Ventry or travel down the road to the beach at Inch for swimming and sunning. Conor Pass is a wonder to the eye—you feel like you're on top of a magical green world, with wonderful water views on each side.

Be sure and take the ride out to Slea Head to see the Blasket Islands, where fishermen lived until 1953. Read the book called *Peig*, by the last woman to live there. It tells of the hardship of their lives. Take the steep walk down to the boat ramp; it's invigorating. Notice the miles of stonewalled sheep pens right down to the sea. Go inland a bit and visit some of the ancient beehive houses made of stones, and the old stone church, St. Malcathair, built in the 600s. The stones are all pale lavender, green, blue, pink, and gold.

Tralee is a charming town. It has a show called Siamsa Tire, put on by the National Folk Theatre of Ireland, that is a winner. The show is full of colorful music, dancing, and mime, so it doesn't matter that it's in Gaelic—you'll understand it all. There is a festival every September that features a "Rose of Tralee," chosen from any country in the world.

Killarney is the biggest tourist town of Kerry and it has plenty to offer. The Irish Tourist Board Office in the Killarney town hall (Tel. 064-31633) can provide you with dates and times of special events in this region. Visit the soft Lakes of Killarney; take a jaunting-car ride to Muckross House or Abbey. The funny drivers have surely kissed the Blarney Stone. Don't forget to see the Gap of Dunloe. The hotels have great Irish musical shows and there are many good Irish singing pubs. Northwest of Killarney, if you hit it just right in August you'll catch the Puck Fair in Killorglan with plenty of step dancing and horse trading. Supposedly it's the oldest fair in Ireland. The Mill Inn in Ballvourney has the best lunch between Killarney and Macroon.

The Ring of Kerry in the south provides a thrilling ride around the outer rim of the Iveragh Peninsula. You'll see lovely farms and breathtaking sea views from high cliffs.

Beenoskee Bed and Breakfast
Mary and Michael Ferriter
Cappateige, Conor Pass Road
Castlegregory, County Kerry
Telephone: 066-7139263
Fax: 066-7139263
E-mail: beenoskee@eircom.net
Bedrooms: 5 with private baths
Rates: €28-30 p.p.; 50 percent discount for children. Vouchers accepted. €20 dinner. **Credit cards:** VISA and MasterCard. **Open:** All year. **Children:** All ages. **Pets:** No. **Smoking:** No. **Provisions for handicapped:** None. **Directions:** From Tralee, take the Conor Pass Road. Beenoskee is 1 mile west of Stradbally Village on the left, overlooking Brandon Bay Beach.

This luxurious, spacious, yellow bungalow sits on a hill overlooking Brandon Bay and unspoiled beaches. It is surrounded by beautiful mountains. Mary will treat you with warm hospitality and will serve you complimentary tea or coffee and homemade Guinness cake. The rooms are nicely situated and decorated, and they have a spectacular view of the seafront, beaches, and the mountains. Mary serves an extensive breakfast menu, including traditional Irish, in her elegant dining room that overlooks the sea. Delicious evening meals are offered with fresh vegetables and delectable home baking. In the area, there are archaeological sites, a heritage center, and museums to visit. There are tranquil walks, surfing, golf, horseback riding, mountain climbing, fishing, windsurfing and swimming nearby. This home is centrally located between Tralee and Dingle, on the beautiful Conor Pass Road. Visit the Blennerville Windmill, Crag Caves, beehive huts on Dingle, and Tralee's Siamsa Tire Theater.

The Shores Country House
Annette O'Mahoney
Cappatigue, Conor Pass Road
Castlegregory, County Kerry
Telephone and **Fax:** 066-7139196
E-mail: theshores@eircom.net
Web: Shores.main_page.com
Bedrooms: 6, all with private baths
Rates: €28-38 p.p.; 33 percent discount for children under 12. Vouchers accepted. €25 dinner. **Credit cards:** VISA, MasterCard, Eurocard.
Open: February 1 to November 30. **Children:** All ages. **Pets:** No.
Smoking: No. **Provisions for handicapped:** Partly. **Directions:** From Tralee, follow Dingle Road for about 10 miles to a junction, take turn to Dingle via Conor Pass. Pass through Stradbally Village, and in approximately 1 mile, you will see the Shores Country House on the left. If you need further directions, please call the owner.

This family-run inn off in the country is a great getaway for city folks. Overlooking the longest beach in Ireland, it has landscaped gardens, and Mount Brandon is in the mountain range just behind the house. The oak, pine, and blue rooms all have wonderful sea views and handsome antiques. There are beautifully extended new Victorian-style rooms in creamy gold and white, all with sea views. There is a superb dining nook with an open fire and a library for guests. Annette greets you with tea and homemade porter cake. Her breakfasts are full Irish, or scrambled eggs and smoked salmon, fresh fruit and yogurt, waffles, croissants, Irish farmhouse cheese. Annette will pack a lunch for you. Her gourmet dinners, featuring fresh salmon, chicken, lamb, or cod, and great desserts are on a menu. Mountain walks are near and the beach is only 10 minutes away. Watersports and horseback riding are available. They now have a lovely, three-bedroom Water's Edge Cottage. AA: 5 Diamonds.

Murphy's Farmhouse
The Murphy Family
Boolteens
Castlemaine, County Kerry
Telephone: 066-9767337
Fax: 066-9767839
E-mail: murphyfarmhouse@eircom.net
Bedrooms: 14 with private baths
Rates: €27 p.p.; 50 percent discount for children under 12, under 2 free. Vouchers accepted. €20 dinner; €13 high tea. **Credit cards:** VISA. **Open:** All year except Christmas Day. **Children:** Yes. **Pets:** Some. **Smoking:** Yes. **Provisions for handicapped:** None. **Directions:** The farmhouse is 2 miles from Castlemaine town. Take the Dingle road (R561) west to Boolteens. A sign will be on the right. Follow the road to the end. There are signs in Castlemaine and Brackhill Cross.

This lovely farm B&B situated on the south flank of the Slieve Mish Mountains was first discovered by us in 1984 and still is a great place to stay. It has been in the family since 1847. When we were at Murphy's, we went to the Puck Fair in Killorglin, originally a pagan country fair where a goat rules as king, and we enjoyed swimming at nearby Inch Beach. At the farm the meals are delicious. The full Irish breakfast, augmented with kippers and various cheeses, as well as the tasty farm dinners, are served in the newly decorated dining room. All the bedrooms have been redecorated with flowered wallpaper and new bedcovers, and now have tea/coffee makers, electric blankets, and electric heaters. The roses and ivy in front, set against the pink house with white trim, make it look like a picture postcard. The cozy and spacious lounge, with a fireplace and television, provides a good opportunity to visit with the many other guests. We found many Irish guests here who come every year. All of the Murphy family pitches in to make your stay here at their ancestral dairy farm a pleasant one. There are golf courses nearby, and walking is very popular in this area.

Ard-na-Mara Country House
Mrs. Ann Murphy
Ballymore, Ventry
Dingle, County Kerry
Telephone: 066-9159072
E-mail: annmurphybnb@hotmail.com
Bedrooms: 4, all with private baths
Rates: €30-35 p.p.; 50 percent discount for children under 12. Vouchers accepted. **Credit cards:** VISA and MasterCard. **Open:** March 1 to October 31. **Children:** All ages. **Pets:** No. **Smoking:** No. **Provisions for handicapped:** None. **Directions:** From Dingle, go by the harbor, continue to the bridge, and then go left toward Slea Head Drive. On the left, 2 miles from the bridge, look for the sign. Turn left toward the water.

This modern home overlooking scenic Ventry Harbor is nicely situated on the R559 for your tour of the Dingle Peninsula. Ann gives you a warm welcome with tea and cookies when you arrive. All the rooms have duvets with tiny green prints and matching curtains. Doubles, twins, and triples are available. All rooms have hair dryers and alarm/clock radios. The lounge is a large living room with a tea/coffee maker, fireplace, television, and piano, so if you'd like an Irish singalong this is your place. A breakfast menu is provided. We noted that French toast, yogurt, fruit and cheese, and other tasty items were included, which will allow you to have a change from the usual cooked breakfast. The chairs in front allow visitors to relax and survey the majestic seacoast beyond. Ann has served for groups of water-color painters from the U.S. who have come with master artists do landscape and seascape painting. It is just that beautiful here, and the Murphys are great hosts. Walking, fishing, golfing, and boat trips are available.

Cleevaun
Sean and Charlotte Cluskey
Lady's Cross
Dingle, County Kerry
Telephone: 066-9151108
Fax: 066-9152228
E-mail: cleevaun@iol.ie
Bedrooms: 8 with private baths
Rates: €34-44 p.p. private bath; 10 percent discount for children.
Credit cards: VISA and MasterCard. **Open:** Mid-March to November.
Children: Yes, older than 8. **Pets:** Only guide dogs. **Smoking:**
Restricted. **Provisions for handicapped:** None. **Directions:** Take the
roundabout (Route 559) in Dingle toward Slea Head Drive. Follow
the signs, keeping the water on the left. Go left over the bridge toward
Ventry. After about 500 yards, the house is on the left with a fence and
beautifully landscaped garden in front surounding the car park.

Cleevaun is one of our favorites. We have been here for many visits,
even before the Cluskeys bought it. We love the panoramic view from
the dining room of fields with sheep, Dingle Bay in the distance, and the
Eask Tower on the hill protecting the harbor. There is a large ancient
burial stone in the field behind the house as well as some underground
tunnels that may have connected some beehive houses. The country
pine woodwork of the downstairs corner room, with the green bedcover and drapes, is very attractive, as are the rest of the rooms, all with
pine furniture and matching bedspreads. In fact, this lovely house is very
nice inside and out, and a good "base camp" from which to explore the
Dingle Peninsula, see the Gallarus Oratory, St. Kilmalkedar, and other
Christian antiquities. Charlotte Cluskey will cook you a wonderful full
Irish breakfast with many choices of eggs, fruit, yogurt, Irish cheese, pancakes, muffins, scones, good jams, and fresh-brewed coffee, including
decaffeinated. She won the 1994 Galtee Breakfast of the Year Award. She
has an extensive library in the fireplaced lounge, which describes the history and sights of the Dingle Peninsula and includes loads of books to
browse through. This B&B is rated by the British RAC and AA.

Cluain Mhuire House
Mrs. Margaret Noonan
Spa Road
Dingle, County Kerry
Telephone: 066-9151291
Bedrooms: 4, all with private baths, plus extra full baths
Rates: €27 p.p.; Discount for children negotiable. Vouchers accepted.
Credit cards: No. **Open:** All year. **Children:** Yes. **Pets:** Yes. **Smoking:**
No. **Provisions for handicapped:** None. **Directions:** At the round-
about in Dingle go right and follow the sign to Cluain Mhuire, as if
going to Connor Pass. It is the second house after Hillgrove Hotel
on the left.

This comfy, cozy B&B is hosted by a lovely lady who will take care of
your every need. Attractive rooms with two doubles or double and single are available. There are nice lounge chairs and umbrellas in the
front garden and the house has a beautiful view of fields and mountains. In the living room there is a beautiful, large fireplace made with
colored stone from Minard Castle. The bedrooms are all carpeted
and pretty, with televisions, electric blankets, hair dryers, irons, and
tea-making facilities. Mrs. Noonan serves a standard Irish cooked
breakfast with choice of cereals and juice, but yogurts, fruit, fish,
beans, or a cold plate are also served. Hot Barry tea and fresh scones
were rolled out for a nice Irish welcome when we visited Mrs. Noonan's traditional Irish home. There is a soccer table game in the dining room and some musical instruments. Take a five-minute walk
into Dingle for shops and restaurants. Take tours to Slea Head, play
golf, go horseback riding, fishing, or on boat trips, and take tour of
Ocean World. Visit the beehive huts and Gallaries Oratory.

The Lighthouse
Mary Murphy
Ballinaboula, Dingle
County Kerry
Telephone: 066-9151829
E-mail: lighthousebandb@eircom.net
Bedrooms: 6 with private baths
Rates: €32 p.p. 50 percent discount for children. Vouchers accepted.
Credit cards: VISA and MasterCard. **Open:** Mid-February to mid-November. **Children:** Yes, 5 and up. **Pets:** No. **Smoking:** No. **Provisions for handicapped:** None. **Directions:** Take the right at the roundabout in town. Then take a left at the end of Main Street and continue to the top of the hill (about .5 km) past Ashmount Terrace. As you descend a little, the Lighthouse will be a yellow house with white fencing, the third B&B on the right.

What a joy to stay at this bed and breakfast with charming hosts Mary and Dennis Murphy. A brief period in Boston inspired this couple's choice of architecture and the use of handsome, naturally finished woodwork throughout. The dining room has a picture-postcard view of Dingle Bay. Each room is spacious with comfortable beds and modern tiled baths. The breakfast menu allows many choices, from fresh fruit salad, the standard Irish fry, or eggs and omelets done many ways. After breakfast, you can take a short walk to the village shops on Main Street, enjoy the craft village, or visit the fishing fleet as they bring in the day's catch. Just to view the surrounding green hills and the checkerboard of stone walls is a thrill. Dingle is very popular, so be advised to book well ahead if traveling in peak season. The Murphys welcome families with young children, as they have two of their own. For recreation, there is blue-flag swimming at Ventry, archaeological explorations, fishing, horseback riding, or a harbor tour to see Fungi, the tame porpoise.

Pax House
Joan Brosnan-Wright
Upper John Street
Dingle, County Kerry
Telephone: 66-9151518
Fax: 66-9152461
E-mail: paxhouse@iol.ie
Bedrooms: 12 with private baths
Rates: €40-80 p.p.; 50 percent discount for children. **Credit cards:** VISA and MasterCard. **Open:** March 1 to December 1. **Children:** All ages. **Pets:** Yes. **Smoking:** Restricted. **Provisions for handicapped:** None. **Directions:** On entering town from Conor Pass, take the first left and continue up John Street for .5 miles. On entering Dingle on N86, pass the racecourse on left, then a red-brick house on the right. Turn right at the Pax House sign.

This beautiful family-run guesthouse has a panoramic view of the bay and harbor. You can watch the fishing boats returning with their catches or see Fungi, the porpoise, cavorting in the water. The lounge with fireplace, dining room with view, and bedrooms, some with views, are spacious and nicely decorated in Celtic themes. The bedrooms vary in color: they are blue, cream, or yellow with off-white curtains with Ohham letters on the side. They have fridges in addition to all the usual necessities. The paintings on the walls are by local artists. The baths are nicely tiled. A large gourmet breakfast is served, with seafood freshly caught in Dingle Bay a specialty, as well as a superb range of meats and cheese. Joan and Ron will gladly share their extensive knowledge of the area. They will recommend the best pub music sessions in town and help plan your visits to the archaeological sites on the peninsula, including Slea Head. You'll find fishing, walking, hiking, golfing, blue-flag swimming, and two equestrian centers, and golfing in this area. AA: 5 Diamonds.

Ocean Wave
Noreen O'Toole
Glenbeigh
Kenmare, County Kerry
Telephone: 066-9768249
Fax: 066-9768412
E-mail: oceanwave@iol.ie
Bedrooms: 6 with private baths
Rates: 35-45 p.p. **Credit cards:** MasterCard and VISA. **Open:** March
to October. **Children:** 8 and over. **Pets:** No. **Smoking:** No. **Provisions
for handicapped:** None. **Directions:** From Killorglin, go south on
N70. The house is 1 km before the town of Glenbeigh on the left. It
is about 7 miles south of Killorglin on the Ring of Kerry.

An impressive country house, set on a hill among landscaped
flower gardens, Ocean Wave overlooks Dingle Bay and Dooks Golf
Links, with mountains up behind it. Elegance and luxury can be seen
in the décor and antique furnishings that appear throughout the
house. The delightful bedrooms are decorated in soft apricot and
peach, cream and pink, and navy. They have canopy beds, hair dryers,
television, and tea-making facilities. Four new full-sized bathrooms
have whirlpool baths. The sitting room and dining room have views of
the bay, and Noreen's specialties in her breakfast menu boast 10 main
dishes. You'll find horseback riding, hill walking, fishing, golf, and
sandy beaches nearby. Singing pubs and a Bog Museum are in the
area. The home has the high AA rating of 4 *Q*s. Be sure to look into
Puck Fair, a real treat in Killorglin in mid-August.

Rockcrest House
Marian and David O'Dwyer
Gortamullen
Kenmare, County Kerry
Telephone: 064-41248
Fax: 064-42253
E-mail: dodwy@eircom.net
Bedrooms: 6, all with private baths
Rates: €27-29 p.p.; 33 percent discount for children. Vouchers accepted. Dinner offered. **Credit cards:** VISA and MasterCard. **Open:** All year. **Children:** All ages. **Pets:** Yes. **Smoking:** No. **Provisions for handicapped:** Yes. **Directions:** Heading south just outside Kenmare town center, there is a sign posted for Rockcrest House off of N71 Killarny Road (on the outskirts of Kenmare town).

Rockcrest House is an elegant, dormer-style guesthouse on a quiet, scenic location overlooking the prehistoric site of a dolmen stone circle and the Kenmore River Valley. A beautiful rock garden and stone wall adorn the entrance to the house. All six rooms are spacious and nicely decorated in bright colors. They have televisions, hair dryers, and tea/coffee-making facilities. Most have fantastic Kenmore River Valley views of the lovely countryside. There is a thirteenth-century arched bridge, the stone circle, and a holy well, all within 800 yards of the house. Marian and David O'Dwyer serve a full Irish breakfast in their attractive dining room, and dinner is offered if booked ahead. Babysitting is offered until midnight. Nearby you'll find golf, horseback riding, walking (including a guided hill walk), tennis, pitch and putt, fishing, boat trips, and all watersports on the Kenmare River. The house is only a 5-minute walk from the town of Kenmare, with its good restaurants and pubs.

Whispering Pines
John and Mary Fitzgerald
Bellheight
Kenmare, County Kerry
Telephone and **Fax:** 064-41194
E-mail: wpines@indigo.ie
Bedrooms: 4, all with private baths
Rates: €32-45. Vouchers not accepted. **Credit cards:** None. **Open:** February 1 to December 1. **Children:** Ages 10 and up. **Pets:** No. **Smoking:** No. **Provisions for handicapped:** None. **Directions:** From the center of Kenmare take Glengarriff Road south. About .5 mile from the center of town, but before the harbor on the right is Whispering Pines, pink with white trim.

This pretty 1914 home, decorated inside with beautiful pastel colors, is a wonderful place to stay. It is located on the edge of town, set behind a lovely garden. John and Mary give you a warm welcome to their home. The 4 spacious and handsomely decorated rooms, all with private baths, are painted in soft colors with matching borders—one in black and pink roses, another with peach walls and matching pink flowered duvets. The home has a comfy, restful feeling. The dining room is spacious, with separate tables. Breakfast is a hearty Irish-cooked meal with homemade brown bread. Dry cereals are available with fruit and other provisions for those who want vegetarian or lighter fare. There is an arched front hall and a nice sitting room with a marble fireplace and television. A 9-hole golf course and a riding stable are nearby for reasonable fees. We walked to town one night and watched a *caeli*. A *caeli* is a Gaelic amateur-night sing-along or dance done in the pubs or local hotels. Kenmare is a quaint town by the sea, not as busy and full of tourists as Killarney, yet more preferred by many.

Carrowmore House
Pat and Kathleen McAuliffe
Knockasarnett
Aghadoe
Killarney, County Kerry
Telephone: 064-33520
E-mail: carrowmorehouse@eircom.net
Bedrooms: 4, all with private baths
Rates: €30 p.p.; 25 percent discount for children. Vouchers are accepted. **Credit cards:** VISA. **Open:** May 1 to October 31. **Children:** All ages. **Pets:** No. **Smoking:** No. **Provisions for handicapped:** None. **Directions:** Leaving Killarney (N22), take first left after Cleeney roundabout. At top of hill, go straight for ½ km.

Set in a tranquil area with a beautiful panoramic view, this bed and breakfast comes highly recommended by other hosts in our book. The bedrooms are spacious, done in rust and cream, peach and brown, pink and blue, and other fashionable colors. All rooms have color-coordinated carpets, linens, and curtains with the color scheme continued in the en suite bathrooms. They have television, hair dry-ers, and tea/coffee facilities. Breakfast is the full Irish-cooked one with eggs any style, both puddings, and grilled tomato. Juice and hot/cold cereals are also served. Save room, though, for the home-baked bread, and sultana scones. For recreation there is horseback riding, golfing, swimming, hill walking, and fishing locally. Pat and Kathleen can arrange local tours from the Carrowmore House.

Chelmsford House
Louise and Pat Griffin
Muckross View, Countess Grove
Killarney Town, County Kerry
Telephone: 064-36402
Fax: 064-33806
E-mail: info @chelmsfordhouse.com
Web: www.chelmsfordhouse.com
Bedrooms: 5 with private baths
Rates: €28-35 p.p. **Open:** January 15 to December 1. **Children:** No.
Pets: No. **Smoking:** No. **Provisions for handicapped:** None. **Directions:**
Follow sign for N71 toward Muckross Road. Take the first left-hand
turn after passing Killarney Avenue Hotel onto Countess Road, then
next right onto Countess Grove. Muckross View is just off this street.

No Vacancy

This luxurious family-run B&B is modern and newly built on 2
floors. All bedrooms are on the upper level and are tastefully decorated
by an interior designer in light blues and yellows, some peaches and
greens, all en suite and spacious. All have television, hair dryers, and
tea/coffee makers. An iron, maps, guidebooks, a pay phone, and the
gardens are available for the use of their guests. Awaken to magnificent views of Killarney's lakes and mountains from some rooms. Choose
from the Griffins' elaborate breakfast menu, including homemade pancakes, plus a full Irish and many other offerings. Chelmsford House is
only a 7-minute walk to town and set on an elevated site with spectacular views. "There are no strangers here, only friends we haven't met,"
is their motto. Golfing, fishing, and swimming on white, sandy beaches
are only 20 minutes away. Hike, horseback ride, or play tennis or
snooker, all within easy reach. The Griffins will help you to arrange
tours to the Ring of Kerry, Dingle Peninsula, or the Gap of Dunloe.

Coffey's Loch Lein Guest House
Eithne Coffey
Golf Course Road, Fossa
Killarney, County Kerry
Telephone: 064-31260
Fax: 064-36151
E-mail: ecoffey@indigo.ie
Web: www.locklein.com
Bedrooms: 16, all with private baths
Rates: €35-60 p.p.; 50 percent discount for children under 12. Vouchers not accepted. **Credit cards:** VISA, MasterCard, Access. **Open:** April to November. **Children:** All ages. **Pets:** No. **Smoking:** Restricted. **Provisions for handicapped:** Yes. **Directions:** From Killarney Center take Killorglin Road for 3 miles. Pass Hotel Europe on the left and Prince of Peace Church. Take the next left on Golf Course Road. Follow the signs to Coffey's Loch Lein.

This impressive two-story guesthouse, located just outside Killarney among beautiful old trees with a large front garden, is made special by Eithne Coffey with her energetic and humorous style. It has panoramic views of Loch Leana, with the mountains rising up to the south, a pretty vista from the lounge and dining room. Snow was on the mountains in May when we were there. All of the rooms have been tastefully redecorated and are beautifully furnished with large private baths. We liked the guesthouse because it is off the main road, set back, and free from the hustle and bustle of downtown Killarney. There are many things to do in Killarney, including the nearby golfing, tennis, boating, fishing, hiking, swimming, and horseback riding. A Dublin hiking club was there when we were at the guesthouse. They were ready to hike the snow-covered MacGillycuddy's Reeks. A delight for many is the trip up the nearby Gap of Dunloe in a pony trap, and stopping for a pint after at the pub, Kate Kearney's, near the entrance. A pint before will make the scenery even rosier. This is a favorite because of the relaxed atmosphere and the charm of the Coffeys, which they are determined to keep, even with new building.

The Grotto
Joan and Jerry Ryan
Fossa
Killarney, County Kerry
Telephone: 064-33283

30 €pp

Bedrooms: 6, all with private baths
Rates: €28 p.p.; 33 percent discount for children under 12. Vouchers accepted. **Credit cards:** VISA and MasterCard. **Open:** March 1 through mid-November. **Children:** All ages. **Pets:** Limited. **Smoking:** No. **Provisions for handicapped:** Yes. **Directions:** Take Killorglin Road (R565—Ring of Kerry/Dingle road). The home is just a few yards beyond Castlerosse Hotel and before the entrance to the Golf Club, 2 km west of Killarney.

A pretty garden greets you as you enter the gate to this beautiful modern country home. The spacious bedrooms with dressing tables are done in Laura Ashley style with colors of peach/cream, grey/pink, and blue/grey, each with its own with tea/coffee-making facilities and television. The dining room has separate tables with white tablecloths and flowers. There is a cozy lounge with a television. Breakfast room opens onto gardens. Breakfast could be a delicious Irish-cooked one with eggs and bacon, or a ham, cheese, mushroom omelet, or a continental/vegetarian one with cereal, yogurt, cheese, and a variety of fresh fruit. Jerry and Joan are extremely helpful in guiding you to the various tourist sights and activities of Killarney, of which there are many and as diverse as any place in Ireland. Killarney's three championship golf courses and fishing club are situated opposite the Grotto on the Ring of Kerry/Dingle road. Horseback riding and hill and mountain hiking are some of the other features. The National Park has hill and forest walks. This B&B has been recommended by many other B&B owners and travelers in Ireland.

Mulberry House
Eileen Tarrant
Rookery Road
Killarney, County Kerry
Telephone: 064-34112
Fax: 064-32534
E-mail: info@mulberryhousebb.com
Bedrooms: 5 with private baths
Rates: €28-50 p.p. 33 percent discount for children up to 12. Vouchers accepted. **Credit cards:** VISA and MasterCard. **Open:** February 1 to December 1. **Children:** All ages. **Pets:** No. **Smoking:** No. **Provisions for handicapped:** Yes, but not for wheelchairs. **Directions:** From roundabout at the beginning of Muckross Road, take an immediate left onto Countess Road, then second right onto Rookery Road. You'll see the sign for the house.

Mulberry House is a beautiful home with two stories, a balcony, and a brick front. The guest lounge is formal, with a fireplace and views of gardens. In front there are unspoiled views of mountains and farm animals. They have a private car parking. The rooms are elegant and brightly colored, and have names over the doors. One has a balcony. All have hair dryers, televisions, and tea/coffee makers. Breakfast includes the choice of standard Irish or different styles of eggs, waffles, pancakes, smoked salmon, and fruit and yogurt. The house backs out into farmland. It is lovely to be in such a quiet and rural area, and yet be only 10 minutes from Killarney center with all its gift shops and entertainment. There is also horseback riding, fishing, hiking, and golfing. Muckross House, Ross Castle, and the lakes are big draws. They are adjacent to the National Event Centre.

Ashgrove House
Nancy O'Neil
Ballybunion Road
Listowel, County Kerry
Telephone: 068-23668/21268
Fax: 068-21268
E-mail: ashgrovehouse@hotmail.com
Bedrooms: 4, 3 with private baths
Rates: €26-28 p.p.; 10 percent discount for children. Vouchers accepted. **Credit cards:** VISA and MasterCard. **Open:** April 1 to September 30. **Children:** All ages. **Pets:** No. **Smoking:** No. **Provisions for handicapped:** Yes, wheelchair accessible. **Directions:** From Listowel town, take the route to Ballybunion (R553). The house is 1 km from Listowel, on the right.

A modern home in a country setting, with breakfast served in a sun room overlooking a garden, is sure to make for a relaxing stay in this bustling market town with its rich literary traditions and colorful shop fronts. Nancy will show you to your comfortable rooms with orthopedic beds, all done up in bright restful tones, and make your visit a pleasant one. Each room has a television and tea/coffee makers. Advice on the historical and recreational facilities, as well as amenities of the area, are offered upon request. The breakfast can be your choice of a continental one or a full Irish one with fresh, homemade scones with preserves. The world-famous Ballybunion Golf course is within 10 minutes away. Also fishing in the river Feale, a swim in the Leisure Center, or just a visit to the local cinema or theater (the Arts and Heritage Center) will encourage you to tarry in scenic and mystical Listowel for a while.

Brook Manor Lodge
Vincent and Margaret O'Sullivan
Fenit Road, Spa
Tralee, County Kerry
Telephone: 066-7120406
Fax: 066-7127552
Bedrooms: 8, all with private baths
Rates: €57-60; 50 percent discount for children. Vouchers not accepted. **Credit cards:** VISA, Access, and AMEX. **Open:** All year. **Children:** All ages. **Pets:** No. **Smoking:** No. **Provisions for handicapped:** Yes, one room. **Directions:** From Tralee center, take R551 and follow signs for Ardfert. Then turn left at R551/R558 junction onto R558 toward Tralee golf course. The house is 2 km from Tralee on the left.

This large, two-story house is "purpose built" on 3.6 acres. It is just outside of Tralee and offers a view of the Slieve Mish Mountains. You will find the O'Sullivans are friendly and helpful hosts. The sumptuous rooms are tastefully decorated in navy and white, or pink and white, with Victorian lamps, chairs, and mirrors. Many rooms look out onto private gardens, and all provide television, telephone, tea/coffee machines, hair dryers, trouser press, and radio/alarm. The breakfast is served in an elegant dining hall by the fireplace or in an adjoining conservatory. Many combinations from the menu are offered, including locally made pork sausages, Irish smoked salmon with fruit or eggs, baked beans or yogurt, cheese and crackers, and freshly made coffee. Afternoon tea is served by the fire in the relaxing guest lounge. Nearby is horseback riding, golf, sailing, fishing, and the beaches are only minutes away. There is also the Siamsa Tire show in Tralee, and there are award-winning seafood restaurants nearby.

Knockbrack
Helen Lyons
Oakpark Road
Tralee, Co. Kerry
Telephone: 066-7127375
E-mail: knockbrackguests@eircom.net
Bedrooms: 3, all with private baths
Rates: € 28-36 p.p.; Single: €40-42. Discount for children under 10. Accepts vouchers. **Credit cards:** VISA and MasterCard. **Open:** March 17 to November 1. **Children:** Yes, over 5. **Pets:** No. **Smoking:** Restricted. **Provisions for handicapped:** None. **Directions:** On Listowel Road (Car Ferry) N69, about .5 miles from town center, the house is about 100 meters from McEllical's Garage (Mercedes Benz agent), on the opposite side of the road.

This new, bright bungalow is in a residential area with cheery gardens and pastoral scenes viewed from the dining room. Some bedrooms are on the ground floor. The large living room is decorated with mahogany furniture and pink furnishings where tea and coffee making facilities are available during the day. The carpeted bedrooms with orthopedic beds are decorated in pink and green, yellow and blue, and peach and green floral patterns with matching duvets and drapes. Helen serves a traditional Irish breakfast with options of hot and cold cereal, fresh fruit, yogurt and home made breads and scones with freshly brewed coffee and tea.. The back garden of Knockbrack borders on a farm where cows can sometimes be seen grazing. This home is convenient to golf, National Folk Theater, and the greyhound race track. You'll find horse riding, fishing, beautiful scenery here and musical entertainment in the pubs. Listowel is the home of the famous Irish playwright, John B. Keane. We have seen his plays in Dublin and in Kilkenny.

O'Sheas
Mairead O'Shea
2 Oakpark Drive
Tralee, County Kerry
Telephone: 066-7180123
Fax: 066-7180188
E-mail: osheasofkerry@eircom.net
Bedrooms: 3, all with private baths
Rates: €28-37 p.p. Vouchers not accepted. **Credit cards:** VISA and MasterCard. **Open:** June to September. **Children:** Yes, 7 and up. **Pets:** No. **Smoking:** No. **Provisions for handicapped:** None. **Directions:** Turn right at the traffic lights at the railway station, coming from Limerick/Killarney direction. After a 3-minute drive, O'Sheas is on the left side. Look for the sign. From Shannon, take N70 south at Tralee station, then turn right on N69. The house is a 3-minute drive away.

This young, hospitable, and helpful couple will make for a pleasant stay in the area. Fran's sister Carol was especially appreciative of the care Mrs. O'Shea took to give them advice on traveling over Connor Pass during daylight hours. This traditional modern home is cozy with family pictures and fluffy pillows in the living room. There is a satellite television and a VCR. The carpeted bedrooms are perfect with curtains, lamps, and bedcovers matching with a Victorian flare, individually decorated in light blues, pinks, peaches, and creams. All rooms have radios and orthopedic beds. The breakfast is either the traditional Irish cooked breakfast or the continental. The side buffet has hot and cold cereal, yogurt, fruit, and juice. The home is close to downtown restaurants and Siamsa Tire (the National Folk Theater of Ireland show). Tralee is a good central place from which to visit the Dingle Peninsula and Killarney. It is convenient to beaches, golf courses, Kerry Airport, and the racetrack. The owners of this B&B run a tour bus company called O'Shea's Travel, which does group and individual tours around Ireland and in the U.K. They also do educational tours.

ALSO RECOMMENDED

Dingle, *Sos an Iolair,* Mrs. Mary Moriarity, Ballintlea, Ventry. Tel: 066-59827. Bungalow in countryside. Comfortable bedrooms, en suite or private bath and shower. Very caring and welcoming couple. Tea/coffee and cookies available whenever requested. Generous draughts of Irish whiskey supplied before one goes out to local restaurant. Recommended to us by Harry McWilliams of Chalfont St. Peter, Buckinghamshire, England.

Kenmare, *An Bruachan,* Julie O'Connor. Killarney Road. Telephone/Fax: 064-41682. E-mail: bruachan@iol.ie Bedrooms: 4, all en suite. Friendly and pretty home in mature garden on the N71. Minutes from town center. Riverfront property.

Kenmare, *Mylestone House,* Mrs. Fiona O'Sullivan, Killowen Road. Telephone: 064-41753. Bedrooms: 5, all with private baths. New luxury residence opposite Kenmare Golf Course. Town center 4 minutes away.

Killarney, *Gap View Farm,* Mrs. Mary Kearney, Ballyhar. Telephone: 066-9764378. Bedrooms: 6, with private baths. It is 8 miles from Killarney town. Send for their color brochure. Recommended by our friend, Marge Brennan of Gloucester, Mass.

Killarney, *O'Mahoney's,* Sheila O'Mahony, Park Road. Telephone: 064-32861. Bedrooms: 6, all en suite. Pleasant home, yellow with white trim, across from Ryan's Hotel. Within walking distance of town center.

Killarney, *St. Anthony's Villa,* Mrs. Mary Connell, Cork Road. Telephone: 064-31534. Bedrooms: 4, with private baths. Especially nice B&B in the Cork Road area. Recommended by many travelers and especially by a top Irish historian, Dr. Edna McGlynn.

Sneem (Ring of Kerry), *Woodvale (Old Convent House),* Mrs. Alice O'Sullivan, Pier Road. Telephone: 064-45181. Bedrooms: 4, all with private baths. Accepts credit cards. Old-World Tudor house set on own grounds on estuary of Sneem River, overlooked by Direenvourig Mountains.

COUNTY KILKENNY

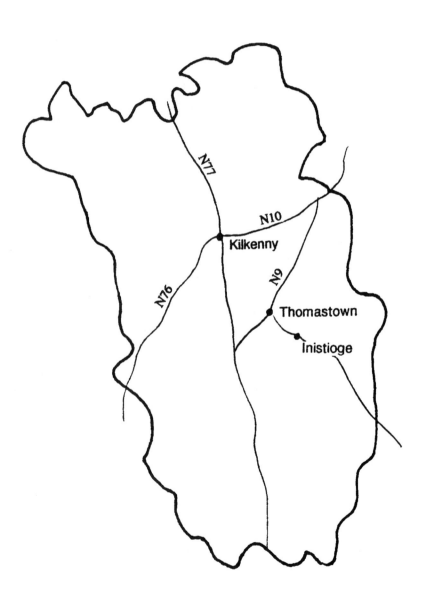

County Kilkenny

County Kilkenny is strategically located between Cork or Tipperary and Dublin, and it's between Waterford and Dublin, which makes it a natural stopping place. It is also only a little over an hour away from Glendalough in the Wicklow Mountains. The countryside is poetically rural, with many sheep farms and the Nore River flowing through the center of the county adding to its scenic beauty.

Kilkenny town, although holding well to its medieval history, is worldly. It offers fine cultural features such as the Irish National Design Center across from the castle, built to encourage young craftspeople. It has a showroom where crafts can be bought, and upstairs is a restaurant with delicious, creative meals. Also, good Irish plays are put on at the Watergate Theater, and there is a cinema in town. You may want to peruse the art galleries and bookstores.

Imposing thirteenth-century Kilkenny Castle, on the river, is the center of attention in this town. Nicely restored with its 2 enormous turrets on either end, it covers 49 acres including a huge public park with playgrounds for children and attractive gardens. You can tour the castle daily, mid-March to September 30 and on weekends the rest of the year.

Go to the Tourist Information Office at the old Shee Alms House on Rose Inn Street at the bridge and join a tour of the town. With a well-informed guide, you'll take a brisk walk to see the Black Abbey; St. Canice's Cathedral; Kyteler's Inn, which once housed a witch; and "Irish Town."

Kyteler's has a fun restaurant downstairs in cave-like rooms. Get a terrific meal at Edward Langton's at 65 John St. It has a high glass-ceilinged dining room and has won many awards.

For a beautiful tour out of Kilkenny town, drive south on R700 to Thomastown, Woodstock Forest Park, and Jerpoint Abbey. Visit the grounds of Mount Juliet House, a hotel on 1,400 acres of pastureland with horses grazing. It has an Equestrian Center and Stud Farm.

Continue through the pastoral country to the town of Inistioge, a heavenly village with the town center nestled among hills and a humpy bridge over the river with sheep lying on its banks. Just across from the park is an excellent restaurant for lunch. The fishing is good in this relaxing area. It is also a pretty ride over to Carrick on Suir and Clonmel in Tipperary.

Cnoc Mhuire
Helen and Don Sheehan
Castle Road
Kilkenny Town, County Kilkenny
Telephone and **Fax:** 056-62161
E-mail: cnocmhuire@eircom.net
Web: www.cnocmhuire.com
Bedrooms: 4; all with private baths
Rates: €30 p.p.; 20 percent discount for children under12. Vouchers accepted. **Credit cards:** Yes. **Open:** Mid-January to mid-December. **Children:** Over10. **Pets:** No. **Smoking:** No. **Provisions for handicapped:** Yes. **Directions:** From Kilkenny town center, at the castle, take Bennetsbridge Road (R700) to the second B&B sign; go right. The house is the first B&B on the left.

This modern bungalow is run by an enchanting couple, Helen and Don, who really put themselves out to make you comfortable and help you with directions for a good tour of Kilkenny. Their rooms are cozy with peach, pink, and rose colors. All have electric blankets, and the bathrooms are good-sized. There is a separate small lounge with a bay window and television. The dining room is quite pleasant and there is plenty of tea and coffee in pots with cozies to keep them hot. Don squeezes fresh orange juice every night, and besides the typical Irish Breakfast, you'll be offered lots of homemade scones, yogurt, fresh fruit like grapefruit, and—some days—kippers. It's a great spot as it is just a short walk to town, where you can visit the medieval castle and park with a playground, and walk around the old city of museums, craft shops, and great pubs and restaurants. We attended the Watergate Theater and saw *Sive,* a fine Irish play by John B. Keane. Golf, fishing, and horseback riding are also within 15 minutes' drive. Be sure you visit The Irish National Design Center for good crafts and a wonderful lunch. Visitors can enjoy playing tennis and walking amongst the scenery.

Danville House
Kitty Stallard
New Ross Road
Kilkenny, County Kilkenny
Telephone and **Fax:** 056-21512
E-mail: treecc@iol.ie
Bedrooms: 5; 4 with private baths, 1 with shared
Rates: €27-30 private; €23-27 shared; 10 percent discount for children. Vouchers accepted. **Credit cards:** No. **Open:** March 1 to November 15. **Children:** All ages. **Pets:** No. **Smoking:** No. **Provisions for handicapped:** None. **Directions:** Find the ring road south of the city. At the roundabout for New Ross (R700), go south for about 200 yards. The entrance for Danville House is on your right.

This stately 1790s Georgian farmhouse situated in a peaceful location just outside Kilkenny will give you a chance to see a 100-acre dairy farm in action. Many antiques adorn the living quarters; one bedroom has a canopy bed (half-tester). Outside there is a large old garden with a swing and farther back a walled kitchen garden where produce and herbs are grown for the meals. The rooms are spacious and provide views of the lush green farm. The dining room has a pretty chandelier over a large antique mahogany table where breakfast is served, a cooked breakfast with homemade breads and plum, marmalade, and raspberry jams. Fishing, golfing, flying, and horseback riding can be arranged nearby. You can do all the sights in Kilkenny while you spend your time outside in a country setting with meadows and tall mature trees. Kitty will set up the miniature croquet set in the backyard for your amusement, or you can tour the cow barn at milking time and observe the inner workings of an Irish farm. It is no wonder that this B&B was a winner of the Galtee Award.

Dunboy Bed and Breakfast
Helen Dunning
10 Parkview Drive, off Freshford Road
Kilkenny, County Kilkenny
Telephone and **Fax:** 066-61460
E-mail: dunboy@eircom.net
Web: www.dunboy.com
Bedrooms: 4, all with private bath
Rates: €28-40 p.p.; 20 percent discount for children under 12. Vouchers accepted. **Credit cards:** Visa and MasterCard. **Open:** February to November. **Children:** All ages. **Pets:** No. **Smoking:** No. **Provisions for handicapped:** None. **Directions:** Call hostess for directions.

   This modern bright and cheery home is situated in a quiet cul de sac, within walking distance of the City Center. One bedroom decorated in greens and yellow with double and single beds is located on the ground floor. The other two rooms are upstairs and fully coordinated using wine, green, cream and pink. The guest lounge is a restful and relaxing room with television, tea/coffee making facilities and an open fire. Helen enjoys sharing her information folder she has gathered over the years describing history and places of interest. Guests can choose from our breakfast menu of a full Irish breakfast with farm fresh eggs, home baked brown bread and preserves. Vegetarians are catered for with a selection of cheese, fresh fruit and yogurts. Recreation in the area are: golf, horse riding, and fishing. Kilkenny has excellent features such as live theater, historic tours, a medieval castle and abbey, an outstanding Design Center, and a brewery which makes a famous ale. Helen can advise you on Kilkenny's great selection of shops, restaurants and pubs for traditional Irish music as well.

Hillgrove
Margaret and Tony Drennan
Bennetsbridge Road
Kilkenny, County Kilkenny
Telephone: 056-51453/22890
Fax: 056-51453
E-mail: hillgrove@esatclear.ie
Bedrooms: 5; all with private baths
Rates: €30 p.p. private bath; 50 percent discount for children under 12. Vouchers accepted. **Credit cards:** None. **Open:** February to November. **Children:** Over 7. **Pets:** No. **Smoking:** No. **Provisions for handicapped:** None. **Directions:** From Kilkenny city, take Bennetsbridge Road (R700) by the castle; the house is 2 miles down on the right, 1 mile from the roundabout.

This lovely ivy-covered house sits on a hill overlooking a patch of beautiful Irish farmland. Margaret and Tony give you a friendly welcome, and their 2 talented daughters play music and do step dancing. Margaret has a good flair for decorating—her downstairs room has small-flowered wallpaper and looks out onto the garden; the others are green and pink or peach, 2 with striped paper; some have antique wardrobes. The Drennans have a handsome Victorian living room with antiques and a television. Their full Irish breakfast is augmented by apple jelly and yogurt, with offerings of French toast or pancakes with maple syrup sometimes. You may also have smoked kippers or smoked trout. The dining room, at the front of the house, has a farm view. You can reach the town center easily, with its castle, museums, and abbey; or try some golf, tennis, fishing, or horseback riding very close by.

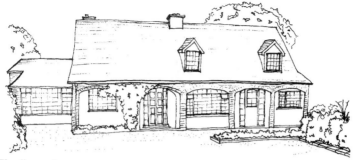

The Laurels
Betty and Brian McHenry
College Road
Kilkenny Town, County Kilkenny
Telephone: 056-61501
Fax: 056-71334
E-mail: laurels@eircom.net
Web: www.thelaurelskilkenny.com
Bedrooms: 5 with private baths, 3 with whirlpool
Rates: €39-50. 20 percent discount for children. **Credit cards:** VISA and MasterCard. **Open:** January 1 to December 30. **Children:** 4 and up. **Pets:** No. **Smoking:** No. **Provisions for handicapped:** Yes, one room. **Directions:** From Kilkenny Castle, turn left at lights at the intersection in town center; go up Patrick Street and turn right after Club House Hotel. Continue to end of road opposite Hotel Kilkenny. Take next turn on right again. The Laurels is on the left.

Betty and Brian and their collie, Jessie, are ready to give you a friendly welcome with tea and biscuits and direct you to Kilkenny's special tourist places, many a few minutes walk from their door. Their remodeled, historic, and attractive home is a quiet place off the main road. The lounge looks out on the front lawn through large picture window. The excellent beds in the pink, cream, and green rooms are perfect for a good rest for weary travelers. All have electric blankets, a television, and hair dryers. Separate tables are filled in the morning with the full Irish breakfast, fruit and yogurts, cheese, eggs as you like, and homemade brown bread, as well as special pudding or various waffles. It's a breakfast fit for a queen (especially in Jubilee year)! Walk to Kilkenny Castle. Nearby are championship golf courses. Fishing and horseback riding are also nearby. The McHenrys are especially good at directing you to historical and cultural features of the region. They were chosen as a Premier Guest House of Kilkenny.

Shillogher House
Michael and Goretti Hennessy
Callan Road (N76)
Kilkenny, County Kilkenny
Telephone: 056-63249/64865
Fax: 056-64865
E-mail: shillogherhouse@tinet.ie
Bedrooms: 5, all with private baths
Rates: €30-40 p.p.; 50 percent discount for children under 12. Vouchers accepted. **Credit cards:** VISA and Access. **Open:** All year, except December 20 to 27. **Children:** All ages. **Pets:** No. **Smoking:** No. **Provisions for handicapped:** None. **Directions:** From Kilkenny City, go 1 km out the Callan Road, past the Hotel Kilkenny.

This fashionable brick house is very new and attractive. Its special feature is the glassed-in conservatory, where you may have tea and chat while enjoying the view of the gardens. The house has a friendly atmosphere. The rooms on 2 floors are modern with gray and pink flowers, peach and navy, or pink and wine colors. An extra bathroom with a tub is tiled in delft blue and white. Tea/coffee makes are in each room. The dining room is stunning and Bill does all the cooking. The large breakfast selection includes the typical Irish Breakfast, baked beans, kippers, fresh plaice, waffles with poached egg and cheese, fresh fruit, cheese board, and yogurt. They are proud of their menu. The B&B is within a few minutes of all the sights of Kilkenny and 1 hour from Cavan. Golf, fishing, and tennis are nearby.

Carrickmourne House
Julie Doyle
New Ross Road
Thomastown, County Kilkenny
Telephone: 056-24124
Fax: 056-24124
Bedrooms: 5, all with private baths
Rates: €25.50-38 p.p.; Single €38.50-48 p.p.; Vouchers accepted. **Credit cards:** VISA and MasterCard. **Open:** January to December 10 **Children:** 10 and up. **Pets:** No. **Smoking:** No. **Provisions for handicapped:** None. **Directions:** From Thomastown follow the signs to Inistioge/New Ross (R700) to the east of the river, for approximately 1.6 km. The driveway is on your left.

This is a picturesque, split-level house on a woodsy hillside above the beautiful Nore Valley, surrounded by beautiful, peaceful country scenery. Julie's husband is a custom builder and it shows. The floors are new pine, all the doors are paneled mahogany, and the spacious bedrooms are really beautifully decorated in pinks and creams, blue and creams, forest greens and rusts. The lot was selected from the Doyle family farm and trees were planted to complement the natural forest. Guests are invited to relax in the private television lounge and browse through the local information brochures. Tea/coffee-making facilities are in every room, as well as televisions. The full Irish breakfast is first rate, with fresh squeezed orange or grapefruit juice and the care of preparation setting it apart from the usual. You can visit Jerpoint Abbey; walk, ride, or golf at the famous Mount Juliet sporting estate, visit local gardens, or fish the Nore or Kings rivers. This is a B&B you feel like visiting more than once.

COUNTY LIMERICK

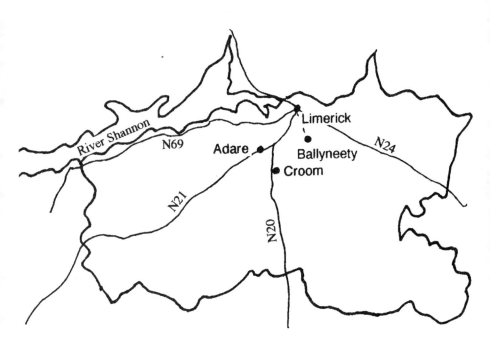

County Limerick

Limerick is a county of rolling farmlands much like Clare and is about the same size as Clare. Although Limerick is the closest large city to Shannon Airport, it's curious that it's in another county. Limerick City is old and charming with good hotels and a theater. It was a 9th-century Danish town. Take a walk across the bridge to the old castle, or peruse the many antique shops, craft shops, and art galleries. The rooftops of the city make a colorful design when seen from the train station. Visit Limerick University on the city's outskirts and see the medieval treasures in the Hunt Museum there. Visit St. Mary's Cathedral from the 12th century on Bridge Street and King John's Castle on Castle Street. The Tourist Information Office is in the old Granary on Michael Street. Bunratty Castle and Folk Park are only 10 miles northwest in County Clare.

Adare is a beautiful village about 10 miles southwest of Limerick. It has a row of shops in thatched cottages and a good selection of restaurants. Many people stay here on their first day in the Irish Republic. Adare Manor Hotel is an elaborate Gothic building on 1,000 acres of grounds and gardens. Inside, heavy wood carvings and crystal chandeliers are a sight. Fifty of the rooms have carved fireplaces. The public may walk all around these grounds for a small fee and visit the Ogham Stone in the woods. There is a fenced-in herb garden, and we met two painters there, husband and wife, both working at their easels. About 30 miles west, over the border in County Kerry, you may want to pay a visit to Listowel, where the famous playwright John B. Keane owns and runs a pub. He lives there and is a great storyteller.

Berkeley Lodge
Pat and Bridie Donegan
Station Road
Adare, County Limerick
Telephone: 061-396857
Fax: 061-396857
E-mail: berlodge@iol.ie
Bedrooms: 6, all with private baths
Rates: €32.50-55; 25 percent discount for children. Vouchers not accepted. **Credit cards:** VISA and MasterCard. **Open:** All year. **Children:** All ages. **Pets:** No. **Smoking:** No. **Provisions for handicapped:** None. **Directions:** Turn right at the roundabout in the Village Centre. They are the fifth house on the right after Texaco Filling Station.

This attractive 4-star bed and breakfast is situated off the main street of the picturesque village of Adare. Made of brick and wood, it offers six pretty bedrooms all with television and tea/coffee facilities. The friendly Donegans make a delicious and full breakfast, and they will help you to choose your itinerary for the day. The rooms are tastefully decorated. Relax in their comfortable lounge. You'll be only three minutes' walk to town, restaurants, the Adare Manor grounds, and historic Heritage Centre. It is close to golf, fishing, horse riding, and pony trekking, and only 30 minutes to Shannon Airport or Bunratty Castle and Folk Park. On your last day, plan to try Irish dinners and shows at the castle and at Folk Park. We did and really enjoyed them. The welcome you receive and the service you enjoy will give you reason to visit again.

Carrigane House
Maura Linnane
Reinroe, Adare
County Limerick
Telephone: 061-396778
E-mail: carrigane.house@oceanfree.net
Web: www.adareaccomations.com
Bedrooms: 6 with private baths
Rates: €30 p.p.; Single €40; 50 percent discount for children. **Credit cards:** No. **Open:** All year. **Children:** Yes. **Pets:** Yes. **Smoking:** No. **Provisions for handicapped:** None. **Directions:** Just before Adare, on the N21, turn left at the roundabout. They are the second house on the right.

This award-winning, spacious, two-story home will welcome guests in the morning. This is very accommodating since you'll often need a nap after you deplane from a night flight at Shannon Airport. The luxurious rooms, decorated mostly in blues and pinks, all have television, tea/coffee makers, hair dryers, and clock radios. Maura's extensive breakfast menu includes French toast or pancakes and maple syrup, scrambled eggs and smoked salmon, cereal, dried and fresh fruits, and yogurts. Of course, she will offer the full Irish also. From this B&B, you may walk to Adare town for a look at Adare Manor Hotel. Very nearby, you'll find fishing and horse riding. The city of Limerick is worth the visit, with their great pubs, restaurants, and theatre.

Castle View House
The Glavin Family
Clonshire
Adare, County Limerick
Telephone: and **Fax:** 061-396394
E-mail: castleview@eircom.net
Bedrooms: 4 with private baths
Rates: €30 p.p.; 50 percent discount for children under 12. Vouchers accepted. €20 dinner. **Credit cards:** VISA, MasterCard, and Access. **Open:** All year. **Children:** Yes. **Pets:** Yes. **Smoking:** No. **Provisions for handicapped:** None. **Directions:** From Limerick proceed to Adare on the N20 to Patrickswell, then N21 (the Killarney Road) out of Adare. Take the second right-hand turn. Castle View House is the second house on the left.

This pretty home is well managed by Colm and Kathleen Glavin and is in a country setting next to Clonshire Equestrian Centre. Rooms are neat and fashionably decorated in shades of lemon, peach, and other pastel colors. There are many amenities like tea- and coffee-making facilities, electric blankets, hairdryers, and direct-dial telephones. Your breakfast can be ordered from an unusually tasty menu listing main entrées such as eggs any style and bacon and sausage, or kippers, toasted cheese, beans and toast, or hot pancakes and maple syrup. These other items besides eggs make this a nice break from the usual Irish cooked breakfast. The dining room is cheery and bright with a view of the garden. We found our stay very pleasant and comfortable. The peaceful and quiet country area makes for a nice respite from the busy village and cities. Golf, badminton, tennis, horse riding, and walking tours are available in the charming town of Adare. Shannon Airport is 35 minutes away. Visitors may enjoy Adare's new heritage center, as well as castles and ruins.

Westfield House
Anne Donegan
Ballingarry Road
Adare, County Limerick
Telephone: 061-396539
E-mail: westfieldhouse@eircom.net
Web: www.adareaccommodation.com
Bedrooms: 3, all with private bath
Rates: €30 p.p.; 25 percent discount for children. Vouchers accepted.
Credit cards: No. **Open:** January to December. **Children:** All ages.
Pets: No. **Smoking:** No. **Provisions for handicapped:** None. **Directions:** Drive through Adare Village. Take first left off N21 onto Ballingarry Road (R519). Drive for .5 mile. Westfield House is the red-bricked dormer on the left.

This lovely modern home is situated in woodland area with beautiful landscaped gardens. Welcoming tea is served upon your arrival. Rooms are spacious and bright and tastefully decorated annually, currently in pink and wine, navy blue and lemon. All have televisions, hair dryers, coffee/tea facilities, and orthopedic beds. Guests have choice of breakfast from a Ballymaloe menu of delectable treats in the separate dinning room. They serve whiskey porridge and smoked salmon among several other choices. Anne guarantees personal attention to your needs. Historic Adare is "Ireland's Prettiest Village." This is a golfer's haven and good touring base. Shannon Airport is only 30 minutes away. Other recreational features are fishing, horse riding, pitch and putt, shooting, archery and the Heritage Center. You will have a peaceful stay and plenty of help with your itinerary.

Lurriga Lodge
Lily Woulfe
Patrickswell, County Limerick
Telephone and **Fax:** 061-355411
E-mail: woulfe@esatclear.ie
Bedrooms: 4, all with private bath
Rates: €28 p.p.; 25 percent discount for children. Vouchers accepted.
Credit cards: VISA and MasterCard. **Open:** May 1 to October 15. **Children:** All ages. **Pets:** Yes. **Smoking:** No. **Provisions for handicapped:** Yes, wheelchair accessible. **Directions:** Drive south from Limerick city toward Adare, on the N20/21. At the split of N20/21 is the Lurriga Lodge sign. Then, 500 yards farther south after Patrickswell, look again for sign on the right. Lurriga Lodge is 200 meters off main Limerick-Killarney road.

This luxurious, Tudor-style country home with palms and garden, patio and play area has been drawing rave reviews from guests for many years. Many travelers return year after year. Sweeney's view rooms upstairs look out on 200 plus acres of scenic farm lands. Pretty rooms with natural wood finishing and meadow colored and floral patterned fabrics grace the bedrooms. Antiques, oriental and African art Michael collected on his globe trotting with British Airways enhances the common rooms. Breakfast is rated by guests as the best in Ireland, the homemade scones are prize winners. Lily and Michael can assist you with your dining plans, visits to local pubs and Irish music, and local attractions such as the thatched cottages in Adare and the Adare Manor hotel. Your kind and gracious hosts will make your stay a memorable one.

ALSO RECOMMENDED

Ballyneety, *Four Seasons,* Mrs. Mary Conway Ryan, Boherlock. Telephone: 061-351365. Bedrooms: 3 with private baths. Credit cards and vouchers accepted. Open January 1 to December 21. It's 7 km southeast of Limerick; 30 minutes to Shannon Airport. Recommended by Judy and Jerry Klinkowitz of Cedar Falls, Iowa.

COUNTY LOUTH

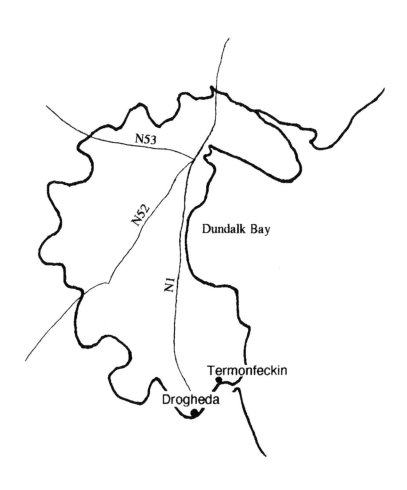

County Louth

County Louth is very small, about the same size as Dublin, and one of its features is that it borders on County Down in Northern Ireland. It also has the Irish Sea along the whole east coast. The Cooley Peninsula in the north, above Dundalk, is a very special sight to see. Begin at Ballymascanlon, take R173, and do a loop around the point of land, stopping at the quaint village of Gyles Quay, and a little farther, King John's Castle. Some of the green sheep-covered hills in the countryside there remind us of scenes in Dingle.

Dundalk is the largest city in Louth. It is a port and has history back to A.D. 600, and has churches and cathedrals to visit. The salt marshes east of the city are home to one of Ireland's best bird sanctuaries and you may spot some very unusual species there. North of town, visit the very curious rounded Neolithic mound called Proleek Dolmen, dating to 3000 B.C.

Industrial Drogheda, surrounded by farms, in the south on the Boyne River, claims a large corner of the famous Battle of the Boyne site. This very historical Viking town dates back to A.D. 911. It was once entirely walled in, and you may still view parts of the wall and the lovely medieval St. Laurence's Gate. Visit Monasterboice with 10th-century High Crosses, and Mellifont Abbey near the Meath border. In the north of Louth, you can drive to Iniskeen in Monaghan, and in the south, you can drive over to see the famed stony tombs at Newgrange in County Meath.

Highfields House Farm
Kitty and Jim McEvoy
Termonfeckin
Drogheda, County Louth
Telephone: 041-9822172
Bedrooms: 3, all with private baths
Rates: €30 p.p.; 50 percent discount for children under12. Vouchers not accepted. **Credit cards:** None. **Open:** March 1 to October 31. **Children:** All ages. **Pets:** No. **Smoking:** No. **Provisions for handicapped:** None. **Directions:** From Drogheda town, take R166 to Termonfeckin, 5 miles northeast. Go down in a vale and over a humpy bridge, and just on the left, see the pub and Triple House Restaurant. Highfields House Farm is just past it on the left at the corner, a two-story stucco with a stone wall and white gate.

This lovely 1725 farmhouse has been in the McEvoy family since 1928. Termonfeckin is in a quaint and picturesque section of Drogheda, while the town center is rather dowdy. Kitty and Jim may greet you in the farmyard; then you will get a cup of tea. We had ours in the wonderful antique kitchen. The house has a handsome big entryway and the rooms are all large and nostalgic, with antique beds and flowered covers in soft colors of lilac, peach and cream, and yellow. The dining room has a fireplace and a large hand-carved rosewood sideboard. The huge lounge has a television and antique furniture, featuring lovely matching Victorian "fainting chairs." Kitty was given an award by Bord Fáilte for Best Breakfast in the county. Her full Irish breakfast includes homemade brown bread with raisins, fresh eggs from their own red hens, fruit, and white or black pudding. Ask about the secret room and the tunnels in the fields; Jim loves to tell the history of the house and town. Livestock, grain, turkeys, and goats are raised on the farm. One mile from the Irish Sea and a sandy beach, this is a good place to visit the Battle of the Boyne artifacts, the Druid site at Newgrange, 2 18-hole golf courses, pubs, and castles of Drogheda.

Tullyesker Country House
Cepta McDonnell
N1 Road, Monasterboice
Drogheda, County Louth
Telephone: 041-9830430
Fax: 041-9832624
E-mail: mcdonnellfamily@ireland.com
Web: www.bestirishbandb.com
Bedrooms: 5, all with private baths
Rates: €29-35 p.p. for a double room. Vouchers not accepted. **Credit cards**: None. **Open:** February 1 to November 30. **Children:** 10 or older. **Pets:** No. **Smoking:** No. **Provisions for handicapped:** None.
Directions: From Drogheda, take N1 north. The B&B is 3 miles north of Drogheda on N1 at Tullyesker Hill. The house is on the right-hand side surrounded by trees.

This marvelous getaway B&B is nested on Tullyesker Hill amid four acres of gardens with panoramic views of the Boyne Valley. Cepta McDonnell's luxurious jewel-toned rooms are lavishly appointed with electric blankets, televisions, hair dryers, toiletries, and tea and coffee-making facilities. The breakfast menu has more items to choose from than any other we've seen in Ireland. It includes such unusual items as a cheese platter with savory biscuits, poached smoked herring with lemon and grilled tomato, Irish smoked salmon and eggs, chicken liver pâté, and what they call a "symphony of fruit," a Tullyesker favorite. Besides these and many different types of eggs, porridge, cereal, and yogurt, there are homemade scones and bread, Bewley's tea and coffee (including decaf!), and Cadbury's hot chocolate. There are tennis courts and walks on the property in the gardens or the woodland. Within driving distance is the 17-foot-high Monasterboice Cross, which has many figures and ornamental designs carved in stone. And just over the border in Meath are the Mellifont Abbey, famous Boyne Valley, Hill of Stone, and fascinating burial mound at Newgrange. The ocean is only a few miles to the east, and the oldest building in the world is nearby.

COUNTY MAYO

N59

Lough Conn

Achill Island

N5

Charlestown

Castlebar

N60

Clew Bay

N60

Westport

N59

Lough Mask

County Mayo

Mayo is another very large county with 2 lakes, Lough Conn and Lough Mask. From Sligo, you may want to take the R313 out to the Mullet Peninsula to the northwest to explore the unspoiled rolling farmlands with sheep and cattle, and its bogs. There is good fishing on the rocks and from the shore at most coastal areas. The town between 2 bays, Belmullet, is quite fancy and modernized. Enjoy the views of sweeping, multicolored grasses of the bogs, and the mystical view of Benwee Head with its stark profile. Farther south you may drive out R319 directly to Achill Island for a look at high cliffs and sandy beaches, and there are pubs with music, too.

You may cut down to the classy town of Westport. It has a nice town center with lots of shops, galleries, cafés, and pubs, and it is very proud of its Sailing Centre. There are some breathtaking views of Clew Bay and Croagh Patrick Mountain, with the huge white statue of St. Patrick standing watch at the top. Here St. Patrick made a 40-day fast, and in honor of him, modern-day pilgrims climb this mountain on the last Sunday of each July.

Throughout Mayo there are a good deal of antique and craft shops. Cong, on the southern border, has the ruins of the Royal Abbey of Cong, Ashford Castle, and it was the town where most of *Quiet Man* was filmed. Knock, a town in the eastern section of Mayo, is known for its Marian Shrine, where an apparition of Our Lady was seen in 1879 at the church of St. John the Baptist. Thousands of pilgrims visit this each year.

Devard
Nora Ward
Westport Road
Castlebar, County Mayo
Telephone and **Fax:** 094-23462
E-mail: devard@esatclear.ie
Web: www.esatclear.ie/~devard
Bedrooms: 5 with private bath (en suite)
Rates: €26-28 p.p.; Single €38.50; 50 percent discount for children.
Vouchers accepted. **Credit cards:** No. **Open:** January 1 to December
20. **Children:** All ages. **Pets:** No. **Smoking:** Yes. **Provisions for handicapped:** Yes, first-floor ramp. **Directions:** Devard is on Westport Road
(the N60), 1 km outside town on the left just after Spar convenience
store.

This is a very comfortable modern bungalow with a very pleasant
hostess in Nora Ward. All bedrooms are fitted with hair dryers, television, tea/coffee makers, electric blankets, and matching bedspreads
and curtains, and are spacious. They are nicely decorated in burgundies, brown and blue with cocoa rugs, and peach with white and
cream duvets. The large baths have bidet, shower, toilet, tiles to the
ceiling in pretty coordinated colors, gold fixtures, and parquet floors.
Devard is set apart in style and decor. One room has a beautiful view
of an anniversary garden of pink roses. Breakfast is full Irish, supplemented with white and black puddings, French toast, porridge,
yogurt, fruit, etc. The brewed coffee hit the spot after drinking so
much instant for breakfast. We are spoiled; we like ours fresh brewed.
There is a handsome marble fireplace in the combination sitting and
dining room. But to us the gracious and genuinely warm Nora Ward
made this home special. This is a good place to stop while traveling
south to Westport. Check out the Breaffy House Hotel for an evening
meal. Golf, swimming, tennis, horseback riding, and fishing are some
of the area activities. The Wards have added a beautiful new entry
conservatory with wicker furniture and garden views.

Lakeview House
Mary Moran
Westport Road
Castlebar, County Mayo
Telephone: 094-22374
Bedrooms: 4, all with private bath
Rates: €27.50 p.p.; 50 percent discount for children. Vouchers not accepted. **Credit cards:** None. **Open:** Easter to end of October. **Children:** All ages. **Pets:** No. **Smoking:** No. **Provisions for handicapped:** Limited. **Directions:** 4 km from Castlebar on the Westport side, on the main N5 route.

This pretty bungalow on spacious grounds has bedrooms all on the main floor decorated in beautiful pastel colors of cream, pink, blue and green. Mary has been welcoming guests to her home since 1973. The cozy lounge has television, and fireplace with a peat fire. Tea and coffee is offered here upon your arrival. Her breakfasts are exceptional with homemade bread and scones. Many of their valued clients return home to try out Mary's recipes. She has had many repeat guests for the past 26 years. Her record of thank-you letters documents this bed and breakfast's high standards. Guests make such comments as, "I award you four stars and an A+"; "These wonderful people deserve the highest accolades for their kindness, warmth, and accommodation"; and "The type of hospitality shown by Mary will certainly encourage more American visitors to come to Ireland." Golf, bowling, swimming, horseback riding , country walks, bicycle for hire, and mountain climbing are some of the recreations available.

Windermere House
Kay and Peter McGrath
Westport Road, Islandeady
Castlebar, County Mayo
Telephone: 094-23329
E-mail: windermerehse@eircom.net
Bedrooms: 5, all with private baths
Rates: €27 p.p.; 50 percent discount for children. Accepts vouchers.
Dinners offered at €18 p.p. **Credit cards:** VISA, MasterCard, and
AmEx. **Open:** January 1 to December 31. **Children:** All ages. **Pets:** No.
Smoking: No. **Provisions for handicapped:** None. **Directions:** From
Castlebar, follow the signs for N5 to Westport. Drive four miles; house
is sign posted on the left. It is set back and painted pink and cream.

This luxurious two-story house, surrounded by neatly kept gardens,
is a home away from home. The amiable McGraths will help you plan
your itinerary. On arrival, Kay will show you to the cheerful guest
lounge and offer you tea or coffee, homemade scones, or Porter cake.
The spacious bedrooms are handsomely decorated in pink, yellow,
peach, and other pastels. Each room has a television, hair dryer,
tea/coffee makers, and a clock radio. A trouser press is on the landing for your use. The bathrooms are a good size and tiled. For breakfast, served in their attractive dining room, you'll find a large choice
and a menu. There are any kind of eggs, with a "Fry," plus yogurt,
fruit, cereal, and cheese. Boats are available for fishing on Bilberry
Lake, 1 km away. Swimming, golf, bowling, hill walking, and the
National Museum of Country Life are all in the area.

Carrabaun House
Angela Gavin
Carrabaun
Westport, County Mayo
Telephone: 098-26196
Fax: 098-28466
E-mail: carrabaun@anu.ie
Bedrooms: 6, all with private baths
Rates: €29 p.p.; 25 percent discount for children. Vouchers accepted.
Credit cards: Access and VISA. **Open:** January 1 to December 21. **Children:** All ages. **Pets:** No. **Smoking:** No. **Provisions for handicapped:** Yes. **Directions:** From Castlebar, you enter on Castlebar Street. Go over the bridge, up Bridge Street, and turn right at the clock. Cross over Shop Street and continue on to Monmument Street. Take a left up Peter Street and continue on Tubber Hill Road. At the back of the hill, turn left on N59 after the railway bridge. After Maxol gas station, look for the Carrabaun House sign on the left. Enter the driveway through the large white pillars.

This neo-Georgian home, with panoramic views of Croagh Patrick, Clew Bay, Clare Islands, and the rolling green fields and stone walls, sits atop a hill just outside Westport. So you have the peace and quiet of a country setting, yet all the many tourist features of Westport close at hand. We found the entry way and ascending staircase of regal proportions. The equally spacious rooms are all very new and colorfully decorated in lime greens, pinks and reds, and one in periwinkle blue with a delft-blue duvet. All have beautiful matching drapes and white dressing tables. You get a bright and fresh feeling. A new bay window has been added to the guest lounge on the first floor. Ask the Gavins to point out the best walks, golfing, bowling, fishing spots, deep-sea fishing, museums, painting classes, and other recreational features of Westport. But come morning they will stuff you full of a tasty Irish Breakfast plus choices of puddings, cheeses, fruit, yogurts, etc.

St. Anthony's
Bob and Sheila Kilkelly
Distillery Road
Westport, County Mayo
Telephone: 098-28887
Fax: 098-25172
E-mail: robert@st-anthonys.com
Web: www.st-anthonys.com
Bedrooms: 6 with private baths
Rates: €35 p.p. **Credit cards:** MasterCard and VISA. **Open:** All year.
Children: No. **Pets:** No. **Smoking:** No. **Provisions for handicapped:**
None. **Directions:** From the corner of South Mall and Bridge Street,
begin on the river side in front of large all-purpose store, McGreevys.
Drive along river, cross over bridge to the left, and turn right. Pass
Emo Gas Station on left, and turn left onto Distillery Street. St Antho-
ny's is the three-story, ivy-covered stone house, two thirds of the way
down on the right.

Built in 1863, this handsome house was once a parsonage called
the Manse. It is centrally located so you can walk to the restaurants,
pubs, and stores of downtown Westport. Private parking is available in
their yard. The rooms, in attractive eclectic décor, are large and have
flowered duvets. Two rooms have Jacuzzis; all have television and
tea/coffee makers. In the large sitting room with a fireplace, you can
chat or play board games on the comfortable chairs.

Breakfast, served in the dining room with red drapes and carpeting, is full Irish, or muesli, cereal and fruit, Irish cheeses and mushrooms on toast, waffles and Boxty, tasty Irish potato pancakes, are their
specialties. There is golf, riding, boating, and fishing in the area. We
had fun walking to the shops, eating at the Urchin Bridge Street Restaurant, and having a perfect lunch at the new McCormack's, upstairs next
to the Stone Gallery. We couldn't resist the double-chocolate and the
rhubarb, apple, and meringue cakes. We walked to a pub that had Irish
fiddle music and singing, very intimate, yet not a lot of smoke.

ALSO RECOMMENDED

Westport, *Glenderan,* Dermot and Ann O'Flaherty, Rosbeg. Telephone: 098-26585. Bedrooms: 6, 4 with private baths. It's 1 km outside Westport, 600 m off Louisburg Road.

COUNTY MEATH

County Meath

Although County Meath borders on County Dublin, the people are as far from the worldly urban style of Dubliners as Irishmen can be. The mystical spirits of the ancients prevail. In this country made up strictly of farms and small towns, history in the form of Bronze-Age tombs and burial mounds swirls about. The Hill of Tara, where most believe the High Kings of Ireland reigned in the 11th century, is just south of Navan. Newgrange, a circular tomb made of stones probably about 1500 B.C., is preserved in excellent condition. A large rock positioned at its opening only allows a thin stream of light inside on December 21 each year for 17 minutes. There are curious markings on some of the stones inside. It's quite an experience to stand inside with a guide, with artificial light and other visitors, and ponder its vast age. Newgrange has smaller lines waiting to get in in September and October. In order to get in on December 21, you must put your name on a list that's backed up a few years. They only escort about 10 to 14 in at a time. Even in summer, you should take a look from outside. The mounds of Nowth and Dowth nearby are worth a visit, too.

There are also more Boyne battlefields to visit in the area. Kids of all ages will enjoy the working Newgrange Farm in Slane, where they can touch every kind of soft farm animal imaginable. There are castles, too, at Trim and south of Navan.

A visit to the town of Kells will round out your magical tour. This is where Scottish monks in the ninth century, in St. Columba's Monastery, wrote, illustrated, and preserved *The Book of Kells,* a Latin interpretation of the four Gospels. A copy of it can be seen in St. Columba's Church of Ireland there in Kells. The original, of course, can be viewed at Trinity College in Dublin.

River Boyne House
Mary Friel
Old Bridge
Drogheda, County Meath
Telephone: 041-9836180
Fax: 041-9836202
Bedrooms: 3, all private baths
Rates: €28-38 p.p.; discount for children. **Credit cards:** AIB and MasterCard. **Open:** April to October. **Children:** All ages. **Pets:** No. **Smoking:** Restricted. **Provisions for handicapped:** Yes, all rooms on the first floor. **Directions:** Call ahead for directions.

This lovely dormered bungalow with pretty garden at front is heralded by guests as" very friendly," "magical," as "one of the best we had in Eire," "warmest welcome we ever had in Eire," and " beautiful." What more can one say? Mary has decorated the bedrooms in cream and green, white pine and blue green, and pink and cream. There is a large sitting room for guests with tea/coffee facilities and television. This bed and breakfast is situated on the Boyne Battlefield of 1690. It is near to New Grange, a huge ancient burial mound that predates Stonehenge. There is golf, fishing and nature walks, and a beach 10 km away. Drogheda is 3 km. Mary was nominated for the Best Family Home of 1997 award. Mary's Breakfast menu is printed in four languages-French, German, Italian, and English. She serves an Irish Breakfast with orange juice, choice of cereal, fresh fruit and yogurt, and any type of eggs, plus porridge on request. The dining room with fireplace and separate tables looks out on green fields with cows and sheep grazing there.

Roughgrange Farm
Irene McDonnell
Donore
Drogheda, County Meath
Telephone: 041-9823147
Bedrooms: 3, all with private baths
Rates: €26 p.p.; Single: €34; discounts for children negotiable. Vouchers accepted. **Credit cards:** VISA and MasterCard. **Open:** March to October 31 or on request during closed times. **Children:** All ages. **Pets:** No. **Smoking:** No. **Provisions for handicapped:** None. **Directions:** From Drogheda take Donore Village Road on the south side of Boyne River. In Donore Village, go right toward Dublin Road (N2). Roughgrange is on your left.

This beautiful seventeenth-century farmhouse B&B is situated in the most historic of valleys in Ireland. It is overlooking the scenic Boyne Valley and is 1.5 km from Newgrange, Nowth, and Dowth. The large living and dining rooms are furnished with handsome period antiques, and with fireplaces to provide warmth and coziness. A full, sumptuous country breakfast is served on a large antique table. Homemade scones, brown bread, black and white pudding, tomato, plus traditional breakfast will get you off to a good start as you visit some of Ireland's most cherished treasures of antiquity—the Hill of Tara, Mellifont Abbey, Monasterboice Crosses, Newgrange, or Kells. Newgrange is the most impressive pre-Celtic tomb. Salmon, trout, and coarse fishing on 280 acres is free to guests. If you like pastoral scenery with sheep and cattle, this is the place for you. If you have any energy left over, golf, swimming, and tennis are within easy reach. The McDonnells will greet you with a warm welcome and advise you of the way to get the most out of your visit to Meath.

Boyne Dale
Paula Casserly
Donaghmore, Slane Road
Navan, County Meath
Telephone and **Fax:** 046-28015
E-mail: boynedale@iolfree.ie
Bedrooms: 5, 3 with private baths, 2 with shared
Rates: €26-30 p.p. private bath; Shared: €23-26. Vouchers accepted.
Credit cards: MasterCard and VISA. **Open:** March 1 to October 31.
Children: Any age. **Pets:** None. **Smoking:** No. **Provisions for handi-capped:** Yes, with help. **Directions:** The house is 2.4 km east of Navan town on the Slane Road (the N51).

This modern bungalow is in the countryside of the famed Boyne Valley, site of the historical Battle of the Boyne. Paula Casserly is bright, enjoyable, and very organized. The rooms—orange, blues and cream, and pink—are pretty with wide windows overlooking gardens. Hot beverage and hair-drying facilities are in each room, and a restful television lounge is available for guests. The handsome dining room has a fireplace, separate tables, and a large window with a view. Choose your breakfast from a menu. It is typical Irish with a choice of beans or cheese; ask ahead for yogurt. Horseback riding is ½ mile away. An 18-hole golf course, public swimming pools, snooker, a race-course, fishing, movies, and gyms are all nearby. They have locker rooms and a cleaning area for equipment for sports enthusiasts. Visit the Dunmore Castle, and September is best to see Newgrange and the Round Tower, 10 minutes away. Other historical monuments are located nearby, including the Newgrange Castle. Listen to traditional music in nearby pubs.

ALSO RECOMMENDED

Navan, *Gainstown House,* Mrs. Mary Reilly, Trim Road (2 miles south of Navan). Telephone: 046-21448. Bedrooms: 4, 1 private bath, but H/C in room. Vouchers accepted. Spacious period-farm residence, pleasantly decorated, on 200 acres. Fishing, golf, swimming, and horseback riding available locally.

Slane, *Conyngham Arms Hotel,* Graham and Bernie Canning. Telephone: 041-9884444. Fax: 041-9824205. Book in U.S. on 800-223-1588, Canada 800-531-6767. Bedrooms: 16. A village inn on main road. The deluxe bedrooms have fourposter beds. Reasonable rates.

Slane, *Hillview,* Mrs. Lily Bagnall, Gernonstown. Telephone: 041-9824327. Bedrooms: 3 with private baths. Vouchers accepted. Just a mile west of Slane center off N51, take road on right. Modern home looking out on beautiful Boyne Valley. Well decorated. Very clean and neat.

COUNTY MONAGHAN

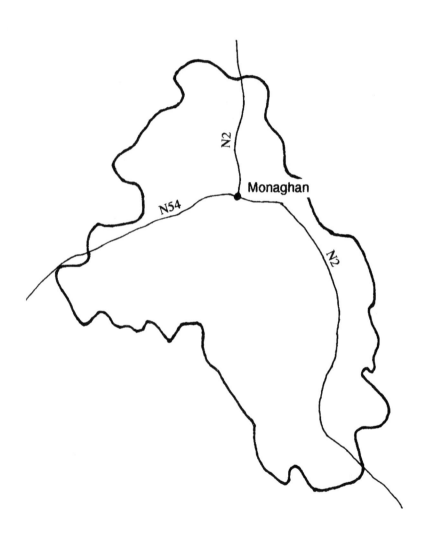

County Monaghan

On entering quiet County Monaghan, you note that there are fewer cars, although the road is wider and the countryside stretches out in wide sweeps of farms. In Carrickmackross you'll find traditional lace, which you can buy at the Carrickmacross Lace Coop. Inishkeen is the birthplace of the celebrated Irish poet Patrick Kavanagh. Monaghan is a good-sized town of fishing fame, is also known for its County Museum, which was an old market house in 1792. Andy's Restaurant in the center of town has good food and service, reasonable prices, and lots of class. We stopped there for lunch and were very impressed. Rossmere Forest Park with its beautiful nature walks and lakes is just to the south of Monaghan town. The town of Clones to the southwest is noted for its Augustinian Abbey of the 12th century with its 75-foot Round Tower, a tenth-century Celtic carved cross in the town center, and the Clones Lace Centre, where you can buy the lace of the ancient craft passed down through the centuries.

Willow Bridge Lodge
Ann Holden
Silver Stream
Armagh Road
Monaghan Town, County Monaghan
Telephone: and **Fax:** 047-81054
E-mail: thelodge@eircom.net
Web: www.homepage.eircom.net/~billh
Bedrooms: 5 with private baths
Rates: €37.50 p.p.; discount for children. Vouchers not accepted.
Credit cards: None. **Open:** January 2 to December 20. **Children:** All ages. **Pets:** Small. **Smoking:** No. **Provisions for handicapped:** Yes.
Directions: Take Armagh Road (N12) out of Monaghan Town. Pass army camp on left, a straight stretch of 500 yards. At Willow Bridge Lodge sign, turn left and go down the driveway, over small bridge. The large bungalow to the left on top of hill is Willow Bridge.

This handsome and spacious motel style bed and breakfast is set in a beautiful garden with panoramic views. The interior has a creative blend of red and blue colors and natural wood paneling. All rooms are furnished with king-sized beds, beautiful natural wood floors, and have en suite baths, televisions with satellite and movie channels, hair dryers, and tea and coffee facilities. There is an inside, spacious, and attractive lounge for conversing with other guests, furnished with a large television and comfortable leatherette chairs and sofas, and an outside patio where you can enjoy nature and the fresh air. Monaghan is the cross roads of Ireland, the main crossing point for ancient Irish kings, where they criss-crossed to do battle. But today, you can break your journey for a peaceful and warm welcome by Bill and Ann Holden. A full Irish breakfast is served.

County Roscommon

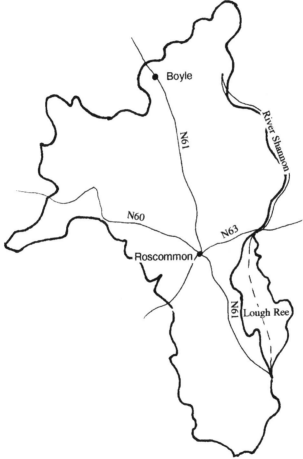

County Roscommon is in the heart of Ireland and is mostly flat plain, making it great farm country. There are just enough boglands, meadows, and low rolling hills dotted with lakes to make it very pleasant to visit. In the north you'll find Lough Key Forest Park, 840 acres with trails for hiking and boats on the lake for renting. There are bog gardens with heather and other small plants to study. Eat at the Lakeshore

Restaurant with picture windows overlooking the water. Very nearby is the town of Boyle, situated between 2 lakes, with the fascinating thirteenth-century Boyle Abbey all in its ancient splendor. This town and surrounding area is a paradise for walkers and fishermen.

The famous blind harpist Turlough O'Carolan (died 1738), is buried at Kilronan Abbey Cemetery, 4 miles northeast of Lough Key. At Castlerea, farther south, is the Clonalis House, built in the 1800s, home of the chieftan of the O'Conor Clan. Here you may view O'Carolan's harp, old glassware, paintings, and Gaelic manuscripts. Afternoon tea is served.

In the center of the county is the historical capitol, Roscommon, a large town where sheep and cattle raising are the main occupations. Visit the Norman stronghold of Roscommon Castle and the ruins of Roscommon Abbey with its 8 sculptures representing medieval Irish soldiers. Northeast of Roscommon city is Strokestown with its Gothic arch leading to Strokestown Park House, built in 1660, a captivating place to visit. This town is also the home of Slieve Baun Handcrafts, sold in the markets and shops all over town.

Abbey House
Christina and Martin Mitchell
Boyle, County Roscommon
Telephone and **Fax:** 079-62385
Bedrooms: 6; 5 with private baths, 1 with shared
Rates: €28-36 p.p. private bath; €25.50 p.p. shared bath; 20 percent discount for children. Vouchers accepted. **Credit cards:** None. **Open:** March 1 to October 31. **Children:** All ages. **Pets:** No. **Smoking:** Lounge only. **Provisions for handicapped:** None. **Directions:** Take N4, Dublin/Sligo Road, to Boyle. The house is .5 km away from town center on the grounds of Boyle Abbey. Turn left R294 and follow Boyle Abbey signs from Dublin. From Sligo, turn right on N61; turn left for Boyle Abbey.

This Georgian house covered with ivy, on lovely grounds between the Abbey and a river, is a delight. Martin and Christina work hard at giving guests good personal service and help with touring. You may want to wander through the gardens or walk to the Forest Park, not far away. All rooms are pleasant and the lounge has a television and an open fire. The Mitchells serve a typical full Irish breakfast. The house is 110 miles from Dublin, midway between there and Donegal. Boyle is only 20 miles from the famous town of Sligo. Walk 4 minutes to town, try one of the two 9-hole golf courses locally, or fish the many lakes and rivers of the beautiful surrounding area. Go boating in Lough Key or walk or cycle in Forest Park. The pleasant hosts will give you all sorts of hints on where to go.

COUNTY SLIGO

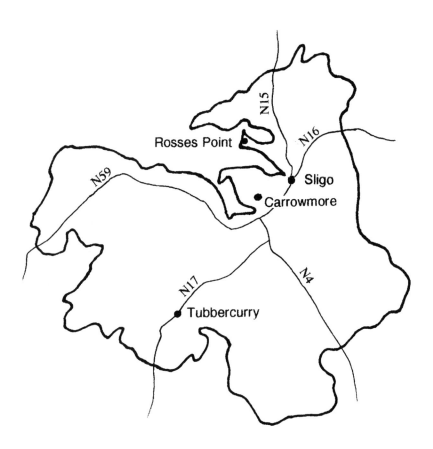

County Sligo

County Sligo is a patchwork of rugged mountains, rolling hills, and sparkling lakes and rivers. The many coves and bays have splendid beaches to enjoy. Starting in the north, coming out of Donegal, you'll reach the wonderful Yeats country right away. You'll see the undulating, moss-green Ben Bulben Mountains and the church spire at Drumcliffe, where W. B. Yeats' father was a minister and where Yeats is buried. The high Celtic cross that he mentions in a poem is here. He called Sligo the "Land of Heart's Desire." Rosses Point and Sandhill are beautiful beaches and the way the sea comes up, you can view mountains, sea, and Drumcliffe all at once. You will be able to visit 60 megalithic mounds and tombs built by Stone-Age man in Carrowmore, outside Sligo town, and in other places in the county. Sligo is a colorful old town with history, good restaurants, art galleries, music, and theater. The Hawk's Well Theatre on Temple Street has good entertainment year round. Lissadel House and Gardens, built in the 1830s, was the home of the famous Gore-Booth family. The Yeats Memorial Building on High Bridge is a must-see attraction. There is also a Yeats signposted country tour of Sligo beauty spots.

Driving south to Tubbercurry, you'll see the breathtaking Ox Mountains and panoramic Ladies Brae. Tubbercurry is the home of the South Sligo Summer School of Traditonal Irish Music and Dance, held every July, where you can learn something about playing the fiddle, pennywhistle, bodhran drums, Uillean pipes, and set and step dancing. If you wish to participate please contact Rita Flannery, Tubbercurry, County Sligo, Ireland, or call her at 071-85010. Don't forget to visit Killoran's Restaurant, which has an Irish party every Thursday night from June to September. Everyone gets a chance to churn the butter, taste the "boxty" potato cakes and hot scones, and sing and dance all night.

County Sligo is a great place for horseback riding (pony trekking), golfing, fishing, cycling, and every watersport you can imagine. You can easily visit Donegal and Leitrim to the north, and County Mayo to the south with its beautiful Westport and the Croagh Patrick Mountain.

Aisling
Des and Nan Faul
Cairns Hill
Sligo, County Sligo
Telephone and **Fax:** 071-60704
e-mail: aislingsligo@eircom.net
Bedrooms: 4, 3 with private baths, 1 shared
Rates: €30 p.p. private bath; €27 shared bath. Vouchers accepted.
Credit cards: VISA and MasterCard. **Open:** All year, except December
20-28. **Children:** No. **Pets:** No. **Smoking:** No. **Provisions for handicapped:** None. **Directions:** From Dublin-Galway: On N4, turn right
at first set of traffic lights onto Cairns Road. From Donegal: Get on N4
and turn left at the traffic lights after the Esso Station. Aisling is the
second bed and breakfast on the left.

The Fauls have a modern bungalow in a peaceful, scenic location
overlooking gardens, mountains, and Sligo Bay in Yeats country. It is
a comfortable family home surrounded by large gardens. The five
rooms are decorated in muted colors of blue, pink, cream, and gold,
and all have televisions, hair dryers, and electric blankets. The dining
room has a beautiful view of Sligo Bay and the imposing, rolling, green
Ben Bulben Mountains. It is surrounded by archaeological sites, a holy
well, lakes, and beaches. Nan serves yogurt and fruit in addition to
her full Irish breakfast. This B&B is surrounded by archeological sites,
a holy well, lakes and beaches. You may visit any of the several beautiful beaches nearby or walk 20 minutes to Sligo town. There are golf
courses, horseback riding, hill climbing, a leisure center, and cinemas
nearby. It's just a short ride to the church and the huge Celtic cross
near Yeat's grave. Visit the Sports Complex in Sligo, too.

Stonecroft
Mary Conway
Off Donegal Road N15
Kintogher
Sligo, County Sligo
Telephone: 071-45667
Fax: 071-44100
E-mail: stonecroft_sligo@yahoo.com
Bedrooms: 5, all with private baths
Rates: €30-44 p.p. private bath; 25 percent discount for children under 12. Vouchers accepted. **Credit cards:** VISA, MasterCard, AmEx, and Diner. **Open:** March 1 to mid-December. **Children:** 3 years and older. **Pets:** No. **Smoking:** Restricted. **Provisions for handicapped:** Yes. **Directions:** Stonecroft is 3 miles north of Sligo town off Donegal Road, N15 on the left side.

Mary Conway, a warm, generous hostess, welcomes you with tea or coffee in her peaceful, spacious home. Her living room and 2 of the guest rooms look out over farmlands to the majestic Ben Bulben Mountains, soft, folded, and moss green like the Pali in Hawaii. The famous Drumcliffe church spire can be seen across the road, and over a large sweep of land to the left you can view the beautiful Drumcliffe Bay. Mary will spend time with you, mapping out routes for touring the area, full of history, where Yeats lived and was buried. The rooms, all on the first floor, are attractive with television and coffee facilities. The matching drapes and quilts are of an unusual modern design in orange and grey or pale green and mulberry. At night, you may eat in the Yeats Tavern, watch television, and visit with her younger boys, David and Mark, as we did. Breakfast is the typical Irish with added fruited yogurt, fresh fruit, and tantalizing hot, crunchy scones. Rosses Point Beach, golf, country walks, horse-riding, fishing. Lough Gill boat trips, surfing, and theater and museums are nearby.

ALSO RECOMMENDED

Sligo/Duncliff, *Rathnashee,* Tess and Sean Haughey, Teesan, Donegal Road. Telephone: 071-43376. Fax: 071-42283. Bedrooms: 3, 2 with private baths. Open March 30 to September 30. Scenic location 2 miles from Sligo town center on N15. Very hospitable hosts who can provide information on archaeological tours in the region.

Sligo Town, *Tree Tops,* Ronan and Doreen MacEvilly, Cleveragh Road. Telephone: 071-60160. Fax: 071-62301. Bedrooms: 5 with private baths. Large and nicely decorated bedrooms. Secluded, lovely home. 5-minute walk to town center.

County Tipperary

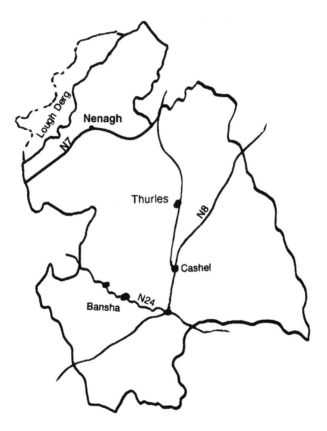

A drive southeast from Limerick Town will take you across rich farmlands through Pallasgreen with its excellent Chaser O'Brien pub/ restaurant, on to Tipperary town, a farming center, then to the quaint town of Bansha in a vale that is surrounded by beautiful hills. We liked this little village and spent some time here. There is an Equestrian Center at the beautiful Bansha House, where racehorses are trained, and where one can experience a wonderful horseback ride through the countryside. One should allow time to take the beautiful drive up the Glen of Aherlow, cross over the mountain on the R662, where there is a lookout with a large Christ statue, and turn right on the I119 to Tipperary town. South of Bansha is the town of Cahir with the beautifully restored, 15th-century Cahir Castle, where tours are available. To the southeast there are the scenic drives to the market towns of Clonmel and Carrisk-On-Suir, sited in an extremely picturesque region. Stop at Kinsell's pub for a pint and a snack, just outside the West Gate of Clonmel when you make your southern swing through Tipperary.

Make sure you visit the famous Rock of Cashel, a steep outcrop of limestone, once a fortress where ancient chieftains were crowned and that later became a Gothic cathedral in the thirteenth century with side chapels. Allow time to have a leisurely visit with a snack and tea at one of the quaint shops near the parking lot before you hike up the road to tour the castle. The area around Cashel is quite pretty and is worthy of an overnight stay. Local shops have the famous Shanagarry tweeds. The Cashel Palace Hotel, a Queen Anne-style building, was once the residence of the archbishops of the Church of Ireland.

Other features of Tipperary are the Kilcooley Abbey, the Abbey of the Holy Cross, and the attractive church at Fethard. Remember the two-day rule. Try to locate a bed and breakfast as a base camp, make side trips from there, and return to your host family in the evening. Its more fun that way.

Dancer Cottage
Carmen and Wolfgang Roedder
Curraghmore
Borrisokane, County Tipperary
Telephone: 067-27414
Fax: 067-27414
E-mail: dcr@eircom.net
Web: dancercottage.cjb.net
Bedrooms: 4 with private baths
Rates: €28-32 p.p; Single €35; discount for children upon arrangement. Some vouchers accepted. Dinner €23 (book previous day).
Credit cards: MasterCard, VISA, and AmEx. **Open:** February 1 to December15. **Children:** All ages. **Pets:** Some. **Smoking:** No. **Provisions for handicapped:** Yes, 2 ground-floor rooms. **Directions:** From south: Limerick N7 to Nenagh. N52 to Borrisokane. From north: Birr N52, Portumna N65 to Borrisokane. Then follow road signs on Main Street to Dancers Cottage.

This comfortable Tudor-style country home is a very quiet place, an oasis where you can relax. It includes a large garden area for guests and all amenities to spend restful days. You will stay in one of their tastefully decorated, cozy, bright rooms with antiques. All are en suite and there are 3 doubles and 1 triple, 3 having a beautiful view of the garden. Enjoy a rich—if you want—Irish-breakfast menu; fresh seasonal home cooking and baking is a specialty. This home has an ideal location to go on many interesting trips, e.g., to Lough Derg—some minutes away—Birr Castle gardens, Silvermine-Slievefelim Mountains, and Clonmacnoise, to name but a few. Golf, pitch and putt, sailing, and tennis are all within easy reach. One of Ireland's most authentic pubs is only minutes away. Have a look at Carmen and Wolfgang's informative Web site, which has many more details.

Dualla House
Mairead and Martin Power
Dualla/Kilkenny Road
Cashel, County Tipperary
Telephone and **Fax:** 062-61487
E-mail: duallahse@eircom.net
Web: www.tipp.ie/dualla-house.htm
Bedrooms: 4 all with private baths
Rates: €30-40 p.p.; 50 percent discount for children. Vouchers accepted. **Credit cards:** VISA and MasterCard. **Open:** March 10 to November 15. **Children:** All ages. **Pets:** No. **Smoking:** No. **Provisions for handicapped:** None. **Directions:** From Cashel, coming from the south, take a right after lights on Main Street. Then take next left, R691, sign posted near church. The Dualla House is 3 miles out on the left with a sign at the gate.

The Dualla House farm and B&B is set in the scenic countryside in the Golden Vale of Tipperary. A Georgian house, it was built in the 1790s by Rody Scully, a local landlord. Going uphill through the entry driveway, you'll see fields full of sheep on either side. Martin and Mairead have more than 1,000 ewes, and they breed Suffolk Crosses and Cheviot Crosses. The guest rooms are spacious with some king-size beds and lovely prints of country scenes on the walls. All have tea-making facilities and grand views of sheep fields. Mairead's delectable breakfasts are comprised of a choice of traditional eggs, sausages, and hams with homemade breads and preserves, a choice of cereals or porridge, fresh fruit, yogurt, and juices. On the property there are farm walks and their colorful, neatly laid-out gardens to enjoy. The Powers are happy to advise you of good spots in the area, such as Holy Cross Abbey, the Rock of Cashel and the famed Brian Boru Traditional Music Show from June to December. Nearby you will find tennis, golf, horseback riding, fishing, and mountain and forest hiking. With lovely open fireplaces, visitors are sure to enjoy themselves at this peaceful, rural retreat.

Thornbrook House
Mary Kennedy
Dualla Road
Cashel, County Tipperary
Telephone: 062-62388
Fax: 062-61480
E-mail: thornbrookhouse@eircom.net
Bedrooms: 5, 3 with private bath, 2 with shared bath
Rates: €32 p.p. with private bath; €28 with shared bath; Single €38-45;
25 percent discount for children. Vouchers accepted. **Credit cards:**
VISA, MasterCard. **Open:** April 1 to November 15. **Children:** All ages.
Pets: No. **Smoking:** No. **Provisions for handicapped:** None. **Directions:** First turn right after Tourist Information Office onto Clonmel
Road. Next, turn left after church onto R691, Dualla Road. The house
is 1 km out on the right. Sign posted near church. Sign at entrance.

Thornbrook House has an excellent reputation for all-around hospitality and accommodations. This elegant country house has beautiful, landscaped gardens front and back. Antiques adorn the
handsomely decorated dining room and guest lounge, both with fireplaces. Thornbrook is within walking distance of the famous Rock of
Cashel castle, and the shops and restaurants of the town. The bedrooms are beautifully decorated with tea-/coffee-making facilities,
hair dryers, and orthopedic beds. An Irish Breakfast is served with a
further choice of fruit, cheese and yogurt, plus baked goods fresh
out of the oven. There is a garage for bikes and a secure parking area.
You will find Mary and Willie experienced in making your visit to the
Golden Vale of Tipperary a very pleasant and comfortable one. Golf,
horse riding, tennis, fishing, and hiking are all found nearby.
Advanced booking is advisable during peak season.

Inch House
John and Nora Egan
Thurles, County Tipperary
Telephone: 0504-51348
Fax: 0504-51754
E-mail: inchhse@iol.ie
Bedrooms: 5 with private baths
Rates: € 52.50-60 p.p. Vouchers not accepted. Dinner offered at €30 p.p. **Credit cards:** VISA, MasterCard, Eurocard, and Lazer. **Open:** January to December 20. **Children:** Yes. **Pets:** No. **Smoking:** Not in dining room. **Provisions for handicapped:** None. **Directions:** From N8 (Dublin-Cork Road), turn off for Thurles. From town centre, take top right-hand side of town to Nenagh Road, drive 6 km and Inch House is sign posted on the left.

This elegant, 1717 restored Georgian manor house was in the Ryan family for 300 years until it was bought by the Egans. The high ceilings, large windows, and lovely antiques will capture your admiration. Stained-glass windows look onto a curving stairway leading to roomy bedrooms with high-back antique beds. The dining room has classic red and green decor, and there is a restaurant open to the public for dinners with prime meats, game, and fresh fish served. The sitting room has a Persian rug, a fireplace and magnificent plaster ceiling designs. Relax here and read or chat. A full Irish breakfast with homemade breads and fresh fruit salad of rhubarb and strawberries is offered. It is only minutes to the Rock of Cashel, Glen of Aherlow, Galtee Mountains, and Lough Derg for fishing and watersports, as well as hunting, horseback riding, and golf.

ALSO RECOMMENDED

Bansha, *Bansha Castle Country House,* John and Theresa Russell, off N24 on right coming south into Bansha Village. Telephone: 062-54187. Fax: 062-54294. Bedrooms: 6, 5 with private baths. Large handsome mansion restored to original beauty, set on large grassy fields with sheep and horses grazing. Convenient for touring beautiful Glen of Aherlow. Fishing and horseback riding available nearby.

COUNTY WATERFORD

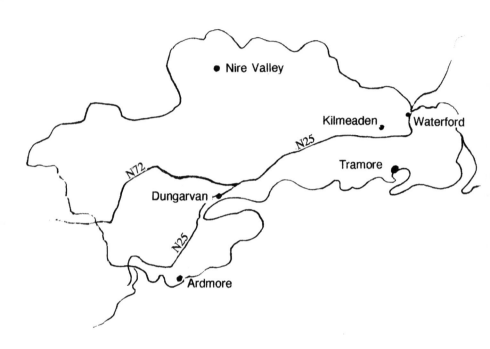

Nire Valley

Kilmeaden

Waterford

N25

N72

Tramore

Dungarvan

N25

Ardmore

County Waterford

Waterford is a small county in the South most noted for its superb Waterford Crystal Factory in the town of Waterford on the eastern rim. The Visitors' Center's lavish displays and the handling of the public are a bit Disneyesque. We were disappointed that we couldn't take photos of the glassblowers as that was quite fascinating, as well as the delicate and careful etching work. We only saw men working there and wondered where the women artisans were. It is a pleasant enough city to see with plenty of medieval towers and old walls. Visit the Reginald Tower Museum, the Waterford Heritage Center, and the New Ross Gallery. The Tourist Office is on the quay on the Suir River bordering the northern edge of town. We had a fine and reasonable Irish lunch at The Olde Stand Restaurant at 45 Michael St. It's a big Victorian place with etched glass doors and inside are cozy benches and tables and a long, lit-up center buffet and carvery with servers. The choices of light or heavy meals were quite varied.

Curraghmore House is a good visit just outside Portlaw. To the east are the rough and pretty Cheekpoint and Passage East with its car ferry to Arthurstown in Wexford, and its water views, wild goats, and numerous water birds to study. Dunmore East, farther south, has picturesque coves and swimming and snorkeling. Tramore, a tourist town on the ocean, has a 3-mile beach and huge amusement park. North from Waterford town it's a straight shot to Kilkenny and northeast it's only 45 miles to Cashel in Tipperary, with its exciting castle rising out of the rock.

To the west, towards Cork, is one of the most charming towns in Ireland, and that is Ardmore. Here, you'll find a glorious sweep of a beach and on the hill is a very high Norman round tower and Celtic-cross cemetery with fantastic views of the beach and the countryside beyond. It's a nice spot to just sit and meditate. There is a bakery on the west side of the main street that is open in summer, where you'll find "melt in your mouth" hot scones and an adorable garden with tables in the back. Back out on the N25, there are some wonderful dairy farms with views of the ocean. Some are bed and breakfasts listed in this book.

Newtown Farm Guesthouse
Teresa O'Connor
Newtown, Grange
Ardmore, County Waterford
Telephone: 024-94143
Fax: 024-94054
E-mail: farm@newtownfarm.com
Web: www.newtownfarm.com
Bedrooms: 7, all with private baths
Rates: €38 p.p.; 50 percent discount for children. Vouchers accepted.
Credit cards: VISA, MasterCard, and Access. **Open:** March 1 to November 31. **Children:** All ages. **Pets:** In shed. **Smoking:** No. **Provisions for handicapped:** None. **Directions:** From Ardmore, take the N25 east and turn south at Fleming's Pub. The farmhouse is ¼ mile on left.

This stunning modern house on a dairy farm in lovely country surroundings has views on all sides of farmland, the Atlantic Ocean, hills and cliff walks. Teresa is very friendly and energetic. She uses a lot of pink flowers in her room colors, as well as blue and green floral designs. Some rooms have balconies. In back of the house, there are farm animals, ducks, and guinea hens for children to visit. The O'Connors also have their own tennis court on the property. The lounge is cozy with a peat fire and the dining room has a pink theme. In her Irish Breakfast, Teresa offers a choice of eggs, beans on toast, and a buffet with juice, fresh fruit, and cereals. There is swimming, golf, tennis, and pony trekking in the area. A children's pony is available. The farm is also close to the sea, handy for fishing. You may easily visit the towns of Ardmore, with its Norman Tower, and medieval Youghal. Bord Fáilte 3 stars, AA 4 diamonds.

Summerhill Farmhouse
Sheila Budds
Kinsalebeg
Ardmore, County Waterford
Telephone: 024-92682
Fax: 024-20916
E-mail: summerhillfm@eircom.net
Bedrooms: 6; 5 with private baths, 1 with shared
Rates: €30 p.p.; 50 percent discount for children. Vouchers accepted.
Credit cards: VISA, MasterCard. **Open:** April 1 to December 1. **Children:** Yes, 12 and over. **Pets:** No. **Smoking:** No. **Provisions for handicapped:** No. **Directions:** On the N25 going east, watch for the Summerhill sign on the left, about 2 to 3 km after the bridge crossing the Blackwater River outside Youghal. Coming west on the N25, it is1.5 km after Grange on the right.

The Budds family will greet you with the most warm welcome you can get in this part of Ireland. This modern farmhouse, with a new lounge with cathedral ceiling and big bay-window view of the Atlantic Ocean beyond the green pasture, is extraordinary. The superb breakfasts are served in the modern dining room with separate tables, and the dinners are equally scrumptious. We enjoyed watching the cows coming up the meadow and the cats being fed the fresh milk. It's a happy family where Sheila manages the bed and breakfast inside and her husband tends the livestock outside. However, it wasn't always that way; as newlyweds, they worked side by side doing the chores. You'll love the comfortable bedrooms decorated in pale primrose, apple white, and pale cream. The baths are tiled in blue and green. Take these side trips: the beach at Ardmore, the medieval walled city of Youghal, and the Blackwater for fishing. Or just relax with a good book in the very beautiful conservatory with a fireplace and pretty blue velvet chairs. Other special bonuses are the pony cart rides around the farm and the miniature golf course by the barn.

Glencree
Rena Power
The Sweep
Kilmeaden, County Waterford
Telephone: 051-384240
Bedrooms: 5 with private baths
Rates: €26 p.p. private bath; Single €38.50 p.p.; 25 percent discount for children under 12. Vouchers accepted. **Credit cards:** None. **Open:** March 1 to October 31. **Children:** All ages. **Pets:** No. **Smoking:** No. **Provisions for handicapped:** None. **Directions:** From Dungarvan, traveling east on the N25, pass the Waterford Coop, go 500 yards farther to the Texaco station. Take a sharp right, go a few hundred yards, and take a right at the sign post for Glencree. The stone-wall entrance is on the right.

Glencree means "heart of the glen" and it is a lovely modern home with a very kind and happy family running it. If you arrive late, Mr. Power will join you for tea and a happy chat until Rena returns from her walk and joins you. You can't help noticing the crystal chandeliers in the hall and the lounge, which is very roomy. They get CNN News on their television. The rooms are comfy with flowered duvets in pink, rose, blue, white, and orange, and green and champagne. One room has a sheepskin rug. A section of the lounge serves as the dining room where Rena will serve you an Irish Breakfast varied with choice of eggs, French toast, cheese, yogurt, and cereal. There is one big table and a small one. They are only 8 minutes from the Waterford Crystal Factory. Beaches are only 15 minutes away and so is horseback riding, golf, and greyhound racing. (One English guest staying at Glencree told us he raised racing greyhounds and had them housed in kennels in Waterford. He loved his dogs and visited them as often as he could.)

Cliff House
Pat and Hilary O'Sullivan
Cliff Road
Tramore, County Waterford
Telephone: 051-391296/381497
Fax: 051-381497
E-mail: hilary@cliffhouse.ie
Web: www.cliffhouse.ie
Bedrooms: 8, all with private bath
Rates: €33 p.p.; 20 percent discount for children. Vouchers accepted.
Credit cards: VISA, MasterCard. **Open:** January to mid-December.
Children: Yes, 6 and up. **Pets:** No. **Smoking:** No. **Provisions for hand-icapped:** Yes. **Directions:** Sign posted in Tramore, off R675, the coast road from Waterford to Dungarvan. Drive through the town of Tramore. Turn left at Ritz Pub to Cliff Road, 400 meters away.

The Cliff house is a luxurious Bed and Breakfast located at Cliff Road with a panoramic view of Tramore Bay. All six bedrooms, including three family suites, are decorated to a very high standard in beautiful pastel colors with television, clock radios, and hair dryers. An extensive breakfast menu offers more than ten choices, such as French toast, apple crepes, and many more mouth-watering dishes. There is a beautiful sunny conservatory with a breathtaking view of Tramore Bay and beautiful landscaped gardens. The Cliff house is highly acclaimed in many travel guides. Recreational facilities and activities nearby include swimming, sailing, tennis, golf, fishing, walking, horse riding, and an indoor leisure center called Splashworld. Waterford Crystal is only ten minutes away. This 4-star home is a delight not to be missed.

Cloneen
Neil and Maria Skedd
Love Lane
Tramore, County Waterford
Telephone and **Fax:** 051-381264
E-mail: cloneen@iol.ie
Web: www.cloneen.net
Bedrooms: 5, all with private baths
Rates: €30 p.p.; €40 single; 50 percent discount for children. Vouchers accepted. €18 dinner. **Credit cards:** VISA and MasterCard. **Open:** All year. **Children:** All ages. **Pets:** No. **Smoking:** No. **Provisions for handicapped:** Yes. **Directions:** Stay on main Waterford-Tramore Road. Go up steep hill, and keep coast on your left. Take next left to Love Lane.

This pretty white dormer bungalow, on one acre, is surrounded by rose trellises and gardens and has secure parking. Tramore is a lovely country section of Waterford not far from the ocean . Maria gives you the Traditional Irish Breakfast with a choice of cereals, scrambled or poached eggs, fresh fruit, and yogurt. Tea and coffee facilities are located in comfortable rooms. There is a large new family room, en suite, with television, tea/coffee makers, and views of the lovely gardens. Also, enjoy the new guest sun lounge. This home is close to golf courses, tennis courts, horeback riding, and scenic walks to the beautiful, golden beaches with many seaside attractions, including a 50-acre amusement park. You can rent a bike in town and discover miles of quiet country roads. The famous Waterford Crystal factory and store is a short drive away. Splashworld, a swimming facility and fitness center, are on Tramore Beach with modern features for all ages to enjoy. Golf and horse riding are nearby.

Glenorney
Marie Murphy
Newtown
Tramore, County Waterford
Telephone: 052-381056
Fax: 051-381103
E-mail: glenoney@iol.ie
Bedrooms: 6, all with private baths
Rates: €35 p.p.; 20 percent discount for children. Vouchers accepted.
Credit cards: VISA, MasterCard, AmEx. **Open:** All year. **Children:**
Yes, 3 and up. **Pets:** No. **Smoking:** No. **Provisions for handicapped:**
Yes. **Directions:** Opposite Tramore Golf Club on the coast road (R
675).

This is a spacious and luxurious home with spectacular views of
Tramore Bay. Pretty bedrooms are done in pastel shades with
peaches, pinks and greens and one room in blue and yellow. The
lounge and dining room is done in pink and green. There is a new
guest sunroom overlooking the bay. An extraordinary home cooked
breakfast menu is served. You have a choice of fruit, cereal and the
Irish cooked breakfast, but your also have a choice of hot kippers with
tomatoes, special French toast, baked beans, or pancakes with maple
syrup. After this sumptuous breakfast, you can tackle nearby Splashworld to use up some of the extra energy. The Murphys will suggest
other recreational options as they pride themselves on attending to
every detail so your stay is enjoyable and relaxing. Marie would like
you to think of the Glenorney as your home away from home. RC
and AA 4 Diamonds.

Sea-Court
Thomas and Elizabeth Moran
Tivoli Road, Tramore
County Waterford
Telephone: 051-386244
E-mail: sea-court@tramore.net
Bedrooms: 6 with private baths
Rates: €29-38.50; 50 percent discount for children. Accepts vouchers. **Credit cards:** VISA, MasterCard, Access. **Open:** February 1 to November 31. **Children:** Yes, over 10. **Pets:** Yes. **Smoking:** No. **Provisions for handicapped:** None. **Directions:** From Waterford, follow R675 to Tramore. On entering Tramore, drive straight through the main roundabout and Sea-Court is the fourth house on the left side.

Sea-Court is a large yellow house in the heart of Tramore and you'll be guaranteed a friendly welcome from the Morans on your arrival. They have secure parking for guests. The rooms are all good sized and have handy equipment, like televisions and tea/coffee facilities. They have a handsome dining room, where you'll find an extensive breakfast menu with 10 items, such as cereal, fruit, yogurt, full Irish, and many other offerings. Relax in the large guest lounge for reading or chatting with other guests. You may also sit in the garden at any time. All the fun of a huge beach, swimming, and Splashworld are at your disposal. Waterford Crystal is only 10 minutes away, and you may play tennis, golf, pitch and putt, or go fishing or horse riding nearby.

Seaview Lodge
Frances and Cyril Darcy
Seaview Park
Tramore, County Waterford
Telephone and **Fax:** 051-381122
E-mail: seaviewlodge@eircom.net
Web: www.seaviewlodge.com
Bedrooms: 4, all with private baths
Rates: €32 p.p.; 20 percent discount for children under 12. Vouchers
accepted. **Credit cards:** VISA, MasterCard. **Open:** May to October.
Children: 6 years and up. **Pets:** No. **Smoking:** No. **Provisions for hand-
icapped:** Yes. **Directions:** Follow the R675 from Waterford to Tramore.
After the Welcome to Tramore sign, turn right onto a small round-
about. Keep left and immediately right into Seaview Park. Watch for
signs.

   This ranch-style bungalow with a spectacular view of the Atlantic
Ocean and extensive gardens has two family bedrooms and three doubles or twins. The rooms are fully equipped with televisions, tea and
coffee makers, and hair dryers. There is a Jacuzzi bath in the main
bathroom with an extra charge. The Darcys offer a special menu that
includes pancakes, omelettes, and smoked kippers or the full Irish
breakfast that is served while overlooking the sea. Nearby is golf, fishing, bird watching, entertainment at night, and you are only 7 minutes from the Waterford Crystal factory. Mrs. Darcy is an exceptional
hostess in every regard. Investigate the sandy beach of Tramore, or
motor to Dungarvan and see some beautiful seascapes. Mrs. Darcy will
advise you on how to proceed and what to see. Splashworld is nearby,
as well as Irish music for visitor entertainment.

Annvill House
Phyllis O'Reilly
The Orchard, Kingsmeadow
Waterford, County Waterford
Telephone and **Fax:** 051-373617
Bedrooms: 5 with private baths
Rates: €23-26 p.p. Vouchers accepted. **Credit cards:** None. **Open:** January 1 to December 21. **Children:** Yes, from age 3. **Pets:** No. **Smoking:** No. **Provisions for handicapped:** None. **Directions:** From Waterford, turn right at N25 roundabout, go to traffic lights, and make a left turn. Annvill is the first on the left.

This attractive, modern, two-story home is very near the Crystal Factory. Phyllis will bring you tea or coffee on arrival in her pleasant lounge with a television. If you wish, she has a video/film available of the factory, plus a 3-hour touring film of Ireland. Her rooms are good sized with some brass beds and flowered quilts in cream, green, peach, and blue. They are painted soft gold, sea haze, almond blossom, and cream. In her dining room, you'll see a glass display case, lit up, with treasures of Waterford crystal collected and received as gifts over the years. Besides the standard Irish Breakfast, she likes to serve potato waffles, the frozen kind. In the area, there is a walking tour of the city, and Irish *caeli* dancing two nights a week. Visit the singing pub, *Mullan's*. Also golf, swimming beaches, fishing, horse-riding facilities, and indoor bowling are nearby. Visit Reginald tower, the only Viking building still in use since 1003. CIE Tours awarded Phyllis the International Award of Excellence, Best Homestay of 1998, 1999, and 2000.

ALSO RECOMMENDED

Waterford, *Dunroven,* Breda Power, Ballinaneesagh, Cork Road. Telephone: 051-374743. Bedrooms: 6, all en suite. Townhouse on the Cork Road or N25. Open all year, except Christmas. Nonsmoking house. Television and tea/coffee facilities in rooms. Recommended by Carmel O'Halloran of Galway.

COUNTY WESTMEATH

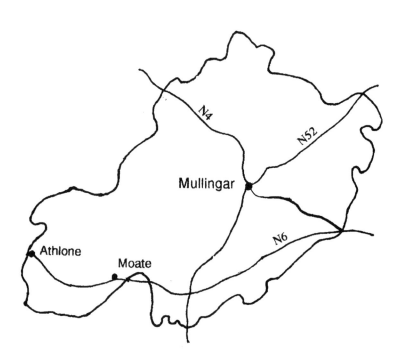

County Westmeath

County Westmeath in the Lakelands area is a perfect place to stay to see the Midlands of Ireland. It is a small county with Lough Ennel and Lough Owel near Mullingar in the center, and it has the great Lowgh Ree along its western edge, which is part of the River Shannon waterway going to the north and south. This is a good county for country walks and bicycling. There is fishing and boating in the lakes and golf in Mullingar, Athlone, Moate, and Birr. You'll find County Westmeath is made up mostly of farmlands, and Mullingar is called the "cattle capital" of Ireland. Much cattle trading is done here, also. In Mullingar, visit the beautiful carved-stone Christ the King Cathedral, and just 5 km south of town be sure to see the Belvedere House Gardens, with its enticing view of the islands of Lough Ennel from its terraced and walled gardens. You'll enjoy the 1790s pub in town called Canten Casey's. On the road from Mullingar to Kells there is a dairy and pig farm that children will adore called the Ben Breeze Open Farm. There are splendid birds to see there also.

North of Mullingar, at Castlepollard, are the Tullynally Castle and Gardens, where the earls of Langford lived, and the Fore Abbey and St. Fechin's 10th-century church in the town of Fore. To the southeast, Athlone is a popular town, being on the N6, the much-traveled road between Galway and Dublin. It stands between Lough Ree and the River Shannon and the views are lovely. Here is where the famous Irish tenor John McCormack was born; and here is where the Irish retreated after the Battle of the Boyne. Visit the handsome Norman 13th-century Athlone Castle and the and the Athlone Crystal showroom. Due east of Athlone is the town of Moate with its golf and horseback riding. Farther east you may explore the interesting and historical Kilbeggan Distillery and Museum. Other houses with lovely gardens to visit are Emo Court, Birr Castle, Clonalis House at Castlerea, and Abbeyleix at Woodland Gardens.

Shelmalier House
Jim and Nancy Denby
Cartrontroy
Retreat Road
Athlone County, Westmeath
Telephone: 0902-72245
Fax: 0902-73190
E-mail: shelmal@iol.ie
Bedrooms: 7, with private baths
Rates: €28 p.p.; 33 percent discount for children. Accept vouchers.
Credit cards: VISA, MasterCard, and EURO. **Open:** January 6 to
December 6. **Children:** All ages. **Pets:** No. **Smoking:** No. **Provisions for
handicapped:** None. **Directions:** Sign posted off the R446 and N55.
Call if this is not sufficient. They are only a mile and a half from town.

Athlone is just about in the center of Ireland, so it is a popular spot
to stop over on a trip across Ireland. This two-story house is a great
place to stay in a very quiet location, with lovely perennial gardens in
the back and front. There is car parking in the rear. It is actually a
dairy farm and you can hear cows lowing at odd times. An Internet
room is available and they hope to have a sauna soon. The rooms
have garden and countryside views. Our room had a queen-sized bed
and 2 twin beds with white and cream lacy coverlets on them. There
was lots of room; a skylight above my head allowed me to watch stars
before blinking off to sleep. One room with a double bed has a yellow
theme, and one has elegant Victorian wallpaper. All have televisions,
hair dryers, and coffee/tea makers. Bathrooms are all good sized and
tiled. Nancy serves a full award-winning breakfast. We walked to town
for exercise and ate at the restaurant recommended by the Denbys.
The River Shannon runs right alongside the town, so there is boating,
fishing, and sightseeing, and golfing and pony trekking in Athlone.
AA 4 Diamonds.

Hounslow House
Eithne Healy
Fore
Castlepollard, County Westmeath
Telephone: 044-61144
Fax: 044-61847
Bedrooms: 5; 4 with private bath, 1 with shared bath
Rates: €27 p.p. private bath; shared €24; 50 percent discount for children. Vouchers accepted. **Credit cards:** MasterCard and VISA. **Open:** March 1 to November 30. **Children:** All ages. **Pets:** No. **Smoking:** No. **Provisions for handicapped:** None. **Directions:** From Dublin, take N4 west to Mullingar, third exit off Mullingsar bypass to Castlepollard. Take the L49 to Fore Village, 4 miles north of Castlepollard, and 6 miles south of Oldcastle. Follow signs from Village of Fore, 1.5 km out.

We don't have many farms in our book, but we have selected a few where you can see a working farm in action, and get a taste of Irish farming. We enjoy them a lot and hope you will too. This lovely 200-year-old farmhouse is located on 100 acres of wooded heights overlooking the beautiful valley of Fore, and its historic abbey. They have beef cows and horses. Two bedrooms have wooden floors decorated in bright colors with pretty curtains, matching douvet covers and pillowcases. Three bedrooms have wall to wall carpets, and are equally color coordinated with hair dryers in the rooms, tea/coffee makers in the bedrooms. Tea or coffee is offered for a real farm welcome on your arrival. There are swings and computers, table tennis and pool tables in the game room. You can visit Tullynally Castle and Lough Lene, and Loughcrew Cairns nearby. An eighteen-hole golf course is also nearby.

Hilltop Country House
Sean and Dympna Casey
Delvin Road (N52), Rathconnell
Mullingar, County Westmeath
Telephone: 044-48958
Fax: 044-48013
E-mail: hilltopcountryhouse@eircom.net
Web: www.hilltopcountryhouse.com
Bedrooms: 5, all with private baths
Rates: €30 p.p.; Single: €40. Vouchers accepted. **Credit cards:** None.
Open: March to November. **Children:** Negotiable. **Pets:** No. **Smoking:**
No. **Provisions for handicapped:** One room is suitable. **Directions:**
Hilltop is 2 miles from Mullingar. From Dublin, take N52, Delvin
Road, second exit off N4 to Mullingar bypass road (not town center). All other routes, take N52/Delvin Road.

This lovely, modern, split-level bungalow is situated in the Lakeland District, is a haven of peace and tranquility. The house has a long porch across the front and terraced gardens. All rooms, comfortably decorated in a mix of antiques and modern furniture, have televisions and original watercolors. The colors are pink and cocoa, rose and white, or pastel flowered. Some have country views or garden views. The splendid gardens, front and back, have a wide variety of trees, shrubs, and flowers. The traditional Irish Breakfast Dympna serves includes a choice of cereals, fresh fruits and compotes, fresh orange juice, and special requests. There is a tea and coffee buffet in the corridor. This house is ideally located as a base for visiting many historical sights such as Christ the King Cathedral and the Military and Historical Museum, or Columb Barracks. There is golf, fishing, and horseback riding available locally. The interior of Canten Casey's Pub, in town, has been kept the same as it was when it began in the 1790s. AA selected 4 Diamonds.

ALSO RECOMMENDED

Athlone, *Harbour House,* Mrs. Bernadette Keagan, Ballykeeran (1.5 km off N55). Telephone: 0902-85063. Fax: 0902-85933. Bedrooms: 6, all with private baths. Vouchers accepted. All major credit cards. Golf, fishing, sailing on Lough Ree, and horseback riding.

Moate, *Temple,* Declan and Bernadette Fagan, Horseleap (4 miles east of Moate on N6). Telephone: 0506-35118. Bedrooms: 8, all with private baths. VISA, MasterCard. Beautiful Victorian farmhouse with lovely garden in parkland setting.

COUNTY WEXFORD

Gorey

N11

N79

Enniscorthy

New Ross

N25

Newbawn

Wexford

County Wexford

Wexford is the southeasternmost county and has a strong tie to England with its ferries crossing from Rosslare Harbor. Ferries also cross from here to LeHavre and Cherbourg, France. Wexford City was a major Viking trading center and is full of medieval buildings. It is quite sophisticated and very proud of its arts and culture centers. They have an Opera Festival for a week every October and enjoy presenting unfamiliar operas. During that week, they have art shows and musical features all over town, a whole program to suit all kinds of people. You should visit Johnstown Castle just south of the city. At Raven Point, across the harbor, is the Wexford Wildlife Reserve.

To the north is Enniscorthy, which has a Strawberry Fair Festival each year at the end of June. You may fish the Slaney River and visit the castle, museum, and famous potters of the area. From Wexford, right on the Irish Sea, drive west to historical New Ross over rolling green hills and farmlands. New Ross is on the River Barrow and has great fishing. The John F. Kennedy Arboretum is a lovely place to visit in this town.

The southwest area has many waterways and at Arthurstown you may take a quaint car ferry across to Passage East in Waterford. Ride down to view the beautiful lighthouse at Hook Head. Two features you can enjoy as a tourist throughout County Wexford are great golf courses and horseback riding.

Ballinkeele House
John and Margaret Maher
Ballymurn
Enniscorthy, County Wexford
Telephone: 053-38105
Fax: 053-38468
E-mail: info@ballinkeele.com
Web: www.ballinkeele.com
Bedrooms: 5, all with private baths
Rates: €70-85 p.p.; Discount for children. Vouchers not accepted. €35 dinner. **Credit cards:** VISA, MasterCard. **Open:** March 1 to November 12. **Children:** Negotiable. **Pets:** 1 room. **Smoking:** Restricted. **Provisions for handicapped:** None. **Directions:** N11 North to Oilgate Village and turn right at sign post. From Enniscorthy, take N11 south to Oilgate village, turn left at sign post. Follow signs to Ballymurn, turn left at sign, it's the second gate on left.

This ancestral home of the Maher family is gray Wicklow granite, built in 1840 by John's great-grandfather in the Georgian style. It is set amidst 360 acres of woodlands and farmland and is stylist and elegant with high ceilings and very large rooms. Soft Oriental rugs grace the front entrance hall and old family portraits and original antique furniture are in all rooms. Some beds are four poster with canopies, and all have farmland views. It has not changed over the years and still has the air of a country manor, although it has all-new central heating. Besides the full Irish breakfast, you'll get yogurt, pancakes, homemade soda bread, and jams. A formal gourmet dinner is served in the beautiful dining room with a set menu. The entrées are 4-star, haute cuisine and must be booked early on day of arrival. The dinner is followed by coffee and tea in the two drawing rooms on a hand-made table. There is croquet, a billiard table, and an all-weather tennis court at Ballinkeele and there are good walks on the grounds and fishing nearby. The town is 10 km away. It is not far from the coast or the tourist attractions of Wexford City.

Cypress House Farm
Nancy and James Wall
Newbawn, County Wexford
Telephone: 051-428335
Fax: 051-428148
E-mail: wallnjc@hotmail.com
Bedrooms: 4, all with private bath
Rates: €25.50-28 p.p. Vouchers accepted. **Credit cards:** AIB, Master-Card, VISA, Bank of Ireland. **Open:** February 1 to November 30. **Children:** Yes, 10 and up. **Pets:** No. **Smoking:** No. **Provisions for handicapped:** None. **Directions:** From Wexford, take the N25 for 12 miles, follow the signs to Newbawn, and look for a *brown* sign post on the left. Stay to the left toward Newbawn for 2 miles and follow the brown signs for Cypress House Farm.

This 1920s two-story farmhouse has a pretty wooden door at its entry. The large windows give you beautiful views of country farmlands. On these 130 acres, the Walls grow grain and hay. James and Nancy are very friendly and James showed us around the big yard where they have a new tennis court with a walking path around it, and a croquet field. The oversized living room has original paintings and we enjoyed tea and delicious scones by a fire in the fireplace. The rooms have good views and are bright and very nicely decorated in ivory, pinks, and greens. Some have Embroidery Anglais; one has a satin coverlet. A new bedroom has a balcony, and there is a new conservatory in the back and garden walks. The dining room has antique furniture and here you will be served the full Irish breakfast, which we hope includes those scones. There is a tennis court on the property. There are equestrian centers, forest walks, golf, fishing, and boating on the River Barrow within 6 or 7 miles. The town of New Ross has many tourist attractions. A pub and restaurant are 5 minutes away.

Ailesbury
Ann O' Dwyer
5 The Moorings
Rosslare Harbour
County Wexford
Telephone and **Fax:** 053-33185
E-mail: ailesb@eircom.net
Bedrooms: 4, 3 with private baths, 1 with shared
Rates: €26.50 to 29 p.p. Accepts vouchers. **Credit cards:** None. **Open:** March 1 to November 15. **Children:** No. **Pets:** No. **Smoking:** No. **Provisions for handicapped:** None. **Directions:** They are a two-minute drive from Rosslare Europort Bus and Rail Terminal. Leaving the port, come up the hill, pass the church, and make a left at bus stop. Ailesbury is the second B&B on the left setback. It overlooks the N25.

Ailesbury is a new house set in beautiful landscaped gardens. The rooms are carefully designed and tastefully decorated, mainly in a beige color. The beds are orthopedic. There is built-in furniture; each room has a television, hair dryer, tea and coffee trays. All are centrally heated. The large bright dining room overlooks gardens to the rear. Their sitting room has soft comfortable chairs for relaxing, reading, or talking. This is an ideal stopover when you arrive in Ireland, and they provide an early breakfast to accommodate guests leaving in early ferries. The house is located within a two-minute walk of 3 hotels, a bank, 2 pubs, and a church. Ample parking can be found in the front and rear, and there is a garage for bicycles and motorcycles. You can find beaches, golf, horseback riding, and fishing within the area. One guest wrote that "Mrs. O'Dwyer knows what guests want and carries out her responsibilities over and above." Another writes, "Of our 500 mile trip through Ireland, yours is the loveliest accommodation of all."

Ardruadh Manor
James Cahill
Spawell Road
Wexford, County Wexford
Telephone and **Fax:** 053-23194
E-mail: ardruadh@hotmail.com
Bedrooms: 6, all with private baths
Rates: €34-40 p.p.; 25 percent discount for children. Vouchers not accepted. **Credit cards:** VISA, MasterCard, Access. **Open:** All year, except 1 week at Christmas. **Children:** Ages 5 and up. **Pets.** No. **Smoking:** Restricted. **Provisions for handicapped:** None. **Directions:** From Wexford City, follow the N25 to Spawell Road and go right. The house is directly on your left; go into the yard and park in the back, opposite County Hall.

This fascinating building was built in 1893 by an Irish timber merchant who saw a house he liked in Norway and had the plans, stones, and wood sent back to Ireland. It has many gables and a handsome wooden arch design over the front doorway. Original doors and windows are Paraná pine. Of the rooms, one has 2 big bay windows looking out to the Slaney River with colors of pink and hot fuchsia in lacey trims. Colors used in other rooms are peach, pastel blues, and green. The Cahills are very cordial. The oversized sitting room has a French ornate couch, a baby grand piano, and other lovely antiques. The red and white dining room has a view of the river. Offerings are full Irish, choices of eggs, tomatoes, mushrooms, muesli, and grapefruit. You'll find tennis, golf, boating, fishing, horse racing and riding, opera, theater, and movies nearby. Also, see the Bird Sanctuary, Johnstown Castle, Heritage Park, and art museums. Rosslare Ferry is 12 miles away. AA 4 Diamonds.

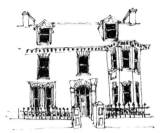

O'Brien's Auburn House
David and Mary O'Brien
2 Auburn Terrace
Redmond Road
Wexford Town, County Wexford
Telephone: 053-23605
Fax: 053-42725
E-mail: mary@obriensauburnhouse.com
Web: www.obriensauburnhouse.com
Bedrooms: 5 with private baths
Rates: €32.50 p.p.; Single €45 p.p; Discount for children under 12.
Vouchers not accepted. **Credit cards:** VISA, MasterCard. **Open:** January
2 to December 18. **Children:** 5 and up. **Pets:** No. **Smoking:** No. **Provi-
sions for handicapped:** None. **Directions:** Take the N25 to Dunnes
Stores in Wexford. After Dunnes, and in front of the railway station,
take the first left to Redmond Road, a street parallel to the river. About
50 yards down and across from the cinema, it is the second red-brick
house on left.

This charming Victorian, red-brick 1891 house was elegantly
restored in 1991 to the highest standards by the O'Briens. Mary and
David take pride in looking after their guests. We liked the high ceilings, large rooms, and Edwardian décor. All the rooms have been elegantly restored and now have televisions and tea-/coffee-making
facilities. One has a fourposter bed. Some overlook the River Slaney.
Soft pastels, used in long drapes, quilts, and rugs, give bedrooms a
stately touch. Large baths with showers remind us of continental pen-
sions. The Opera Festival was on when we were there, and met a couple
from England who had researched all the B&Bs in Wexford and picked
this one. The young couple are a delight and anxious to please. Their
breakfast is served in a large dining room through glass doors off the
fireplaced lounge. The breakfast is the full Irish one but cereals, yogurts,
cheeses, and a choice of eggs are available for vegetarians. Amenities
within short distances are the Blue Flag beaches, golf, horseback riding, swimming, golfing, bird sanctuary, scenic and historic walks, Heritage Park, and Johnstown Castle. The house has a private car park.

ALSO RECOMMENDED

New Ross, *Rosville House,* Philomena Gallagher, off N25, 1 km from New Ross on the Wexford Road. Telephone 051-421798. Bedrooms: 5, 4 with private baths. Modern bungalow in Knockmullen set on the hillside overlooking Barrow River Valley. Nice border of roses in front. Car park in rear. Sunny breakfast room when we were there. Pleasant hostess.

COUNTY WICKLOW

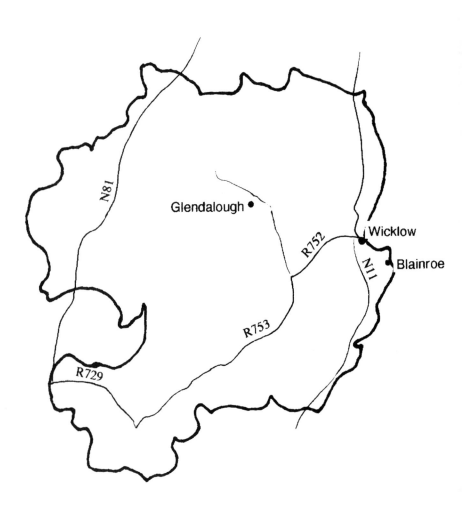

County Wicklow

County Wicklow is unique and notable especially for its starring feature of the wooded Glendalough Mountains and Valley, and the seventh- to fourteenth-century ruins of St. Kevin's Monastery. With its chapel, cathedral, round tower, and fine old Celtic crosses laid out over acres of greenery, it is awe inspiring. Its new Visitor Center informs you of the whole history with films, models, and pictures.

The other special feature of this county is its location so central to Dublin, Kilkenny, and the coast, and it contains the direct route to County Wexford in the south. Wicklow town, right on the Irish Sea, has ruins and castles of its own in addition to good beaches. South of Wicklow and Glendalough, at Avondale Forest Park, is a peaceful place called "Meeting of the Waters," named for a poem of Thomas Moore, where you may hear traditional Irish music every day in season. Here you may visit Avondale House, the home of the great Irish patriot, Charles Parnell. Visit the extensive Powerscourt Gardens, the pride of Wicklow.

In the same area is the town of Avoca, home of Avoca Handwoven Woolen Goods. At the Craft Shop, you may watch a weaver working at his or her loom. Working further south you'll enjoy the boats and quays of the fishing town of Arklow. Visit the Arklow Pottery Factory and Craft Shop. Take a walk on Brittas Bay Beach and visit the Maritime Museum.

In the northwest corner of the county is the tiny town of Russborough on a lake which proudly displays the Russborough House, an elaborate baroque, granite house, built in the 1740s, which has paintings by famous European artists. Ashford, to the north of Wicklow town, is known for its lovely Mount Usher Gardens abloom with azaleas and rhododendrons in the spring. Traveling northeast, you'll want to take the marvelous refreshing hilltop walk along Bray Head with its panoramic ocean views.

Ballyknocken House
Catherine Byrne-Fulvio
Glenealy, Ashford
County Wicklow
Telephone: 0404-44627
Fax: 0404-44696
E-mail: cfulvio@ballknocken.com
Bedrooms: 7 with private baths
Rates: €40-50 p.p.; 25 percent discount for children. Vouchers not accepted. Dinner offered by prior arrangement: €28 p.p. **Credit cards:** VISA and MasterCard. **Open:** March 1 to November 30. **Children:** All ages. **Pets:** No. **Smoking:** No. **Provisions for handicapped:** None.
Directions: Follow the N11 (main Dublin-Wicklow-Wexford road) to Ashford. Turn right after Chester Beatty Pub. Continue for 3.5 miles. Ballyknocken is on the right.

A colorful rose garden greets guests arriving at this distinctive, ivy-covered 1850 Victorian farmhouse. The bedrooms and the rest of the house are furnished with Victorian-period antiques and family memorabilia, as this house has charmed guests for three generations. Ask the hostess to tell you their rich ancestral stories, and ask about the fascinating ghosts. All the rooms have televisions, hairdryers, direct-dial phones, clock radios, and tea/coffee makers. There is a Victorian lounge with an open fireplace. Their award-winning breakfasts consist of a full Irish with a buffet. Their specialty is Hot Drop Scones with honey and chopped nuts. If planned ahead, Catherine would be pleased to share soda-bread recipes and show guests how to cook Irish meals. They offer a seven-day walking package, wherein they transport guests, along with a hearty lunch, to hikes across heathery moors, by lakes, and over mountains. They end up at a nearby village where they are picked up at end of day. Close to Glendalough and Avoca, Powerscourt and golf. AA awarded them 4 Diamonds.

Greenfields
Conor Moloney
Blainroe, County Wicklow
Telephone: 0404-68309
Bedrooms: 5, all with private baths
Rates: €23-25 p.p.; 50 percent discount for children. Vouchers not accepted. **Credit cards:** VISA, MasterCard. **Open:** January 1 to December 31. **Children:** All ages. **Pets:** Yes. **Smoking:** Yes. **Provisions for handicapped:** Yes, wheelchair accessible. **Directions:** Go 5 miles out on coast road (Dunbar Road), south of Wicklow town. Greenfields is the first house on left after Blainroe Golf Club, on the sea side.

This beautiful ranch-style bungalow stands on one and half acres, with a spring pond in the garden, in a gorgeous setting with views of the ocean. There is a nice sunny guest lounge where tea or coffee is served. The rooms are beautifully decorated in blues and greens, pinks, or blue and white. Guests may also use the sunroom facing the Irish sea, or the game room with pool table. There is an extensive breakfast menu, served in their handsome dining room, that includes the full Irish breakfast plus cheeses, yogurts, both puddings, peppered mackerel, and smoked kippers. Go to the beach or sun in the garden, play golf at the championship course next door, fish for sea fish or trout, go horseback riding 10 km away, take walks downtown, and by all means, go hear the traditional Irish music played daily at the Meeting of the Waters near Avondale, 8 miles south of town. Avondale is the home of the famous Irish patriot, Charles Parnell. Donald Hunt, author of *To the Greenfields Beyond* has stayed here.

Carmel's
Carmel Hawkins
Annamoe
Glendalough, County Wicklow
Telephone: and **Fax:** 0404-45297
E-mail: carmelsbandb@eircom.net
Web: www.homepage.eircom.net1~carmels
Bedrooms: 4 with private baths
Rates: €28 p.p.; 25 percent discount for children. Vouchers not accepted. **Credit cards:** None. **Open:** March 1 to November 15. **Children:** All ages. **Pets:** No. **Smoking:** No. **Provisions for handicapped:** Yes. **Directions:** From Dublin, take the N11 to the sign post for Glendalough. Go to Laragh Village, and take a left to Annamoe. Follow the finger-post sign to Carmel's or ask at any shop in Annamoe.

This home is family run and has been extended to make rooms for the B&B. The Hawkinses are known for their hospitality and congeniality. Set in the heart of the breathtaking Wicklow Mountains, this B&B will give you a break from the hustle and bustle of cities. All the rooms are larger now, and tastefully decorated with a personal touch. Fresh flowers adorn them and for that homey feeling, Carmel has electric blankets and hairdryers for each room. The lounge has a television and it has been extended. In the dining room you will be given a real Irish breakfast along with different ideas like fresh fruit salad, home-baked muffins, and cheeses of different countries. The B&B is only 1 hour to the ferry to England, 1½ hours to Dublin City, and 17 miles to Bray Head. It is close to Avoca, home of *Ballykissangel* and only 7 miles to the well-known mountains and woods of the splendid Glendalough, with its monastic ruins in the valley, ancient chapel, round tower, and numbers of Celtic crosses. Some of the ruins date back to the seventh century, when St. Kevin founded the monastery. Don't miss this awesome sight. Visit famed Powerscourt Gardens and Blessington lakes nearby. You may also golf and fish nearby.

Rosita
Rita Byrne
Dunbur Park
Wicklow Town, County Wicklow
Telephone: 0404-67059
Bedrooms: 4, all with private baths
Rates: €30 p.p. 20 percent discount for children. Vouchers accepted.
Credit cards: None. **Open:** March 1 to October 31. **Children:** Yes.
Pets: No. **Smoking:** No. **Provisions for handicapped:** None. **Directions:** Drive through town center, pass Billy Boyne's monument, on to Dunbur Road. At pedestrian crossing, turn right into Dunbur Park. The B&B is the last bungalow on right.

A warm welcome greets you at this friendly modern Georgian bungalow overlooking Wicklow Bay, where Rita and her husband George have been hosting B&B guests for over 20 years. This is a popular place with many Irish travelers, returning each year. It is surrounded by a lovely garden where the garden motif continues into the home with lovely lemon, lavender, cream, pale blue and pink flowered bedrooms, which now have televisions. The lounge has a large television where tea, coffee, and hot scones with homemade jam are served. The dining room has separate tables with nice mahogany furniture looking out onto patio and garden. A full Irish breakfast is served with additional items such as cheeses, yogurts, fresh fruit , porridge and cereals. Here you will be treated as family. Rita notes that the old refurbished Gaol is worth a visit. It is open 10 A.M. to 5 P.M. It takes you back to 1700/1800. Other recreational features are golf, tennis, swimming, horse riding, fishing, and snooker.

ALSO RECOMMENDED

Coolgreaney, *Ballykilty Farmhouse,* Mrs. A Nuzum. From Arklow, take Coolgreaney Road at the roundabout and follow the same road for three miles. Ballykilty is the yellow farmhouse on the right. Telephone: 0402-37111. Beautiful, peaceful garden surrounds house. Old-fashioned fireplace in dining room. Won Farmhouse of the Year Award. Working dairy farm with other farm animals in rear pasture. Mrs. Nuzum is a pleasant and accommodating host.

Northern Ireland

NORTHERN IRELAND

Introduction to Northern Ireland

BACKGROUND

One cannot really speak of Northern Ireland as being separate from the Republic. There are so many traditions, common heritages, and histories that bind these countries and people together. Currently, there is a genuine, common hope for peace and future prosperity on both sides of the border. We are encouraged by recent developments that reveal that the Unionists and the Republicans in the North are moving ahead to build a lasting peace.

One need not be afraid. Northern Ireland is presently very peaceful with a few isolated incidents, none of which threatened life or limb. The people are exceptionally warm, friendly, and helpful. You should not hesitate to visit Ulster. It is perfectly safe! It's like an Irish country with a British mix of customs, currency, and culture—a hybrid of sorts. This gives Northern Ireland its own interesting charm. You will be impressed by the romantic beauty of the Glens of Antrim where the mountains roll down to the sea, which hides crescent-shaped sandy swimming beaches and spectacular vistas. At one bed and breakfast on a hill above Cushendall we could look across the Irish Sea and see the Mull of Kintyre, part of Scotland—15 miles away!

One should be cautious of generalizing about the Northern Irish. You find here two predominant groups: the Irish catholics, a minority in Ulster; and the Scots and English, who are most numerous. The Scots brought their Protestant religion with them, which in most cases is rooted in Presbyterianism. The English traditionally belong to the Church of England, which is Episcopalian. This religious difference was thought by many to be at the heart of the conflict in Northern Ireland, but there have been some convincing arguments that a criminal element has benefited from the troubles through drug dealing and gun running. The United States has strongly supported programs in both Eire and the North to curb the radicals on both sides by offering economic assistance to create jobs, especially in Belfast and Londonderry.

One is struck by the irony of seeing the beautiful Ulster cities and countryside and imaging this place as a batttleground.

We recommend the book cited in our "Introduction to Ireland" at the beginnning of this book, Edmund Curtis' *A History of Ireland,* if you wish to explore the roots of this problem in more depth. His is one of the most popular and authoritative historical accounts up through 1922. It will help you to understand the difficulties the Irish face in achieving a lasting peace.

We found the operators of B&Bs in the North to be more conservative and cautious. While all were very friendly, we don't know if their reluctance to be in our book was due to their business acumen or because of the troubles they have endured since the early 1970s. We must explain that when we asked the hosts if they wanted to be in the book after we had inspected the premises, it took a lot more explaining than it did in the Republic of Ireland. We attribute some of this to the rapid changes occuring in people's lives in Northern Ireland. Northern Ireland does not have a *national* Town and Country Homes Association like the Republic of Ireland does. Tourism is organized more by region and county. When we were in Londonderry last June, the Northern Ireland Tourist Board branch office was out of copies of a helpful booklet describing coastal B&Bs, The Town & Seaside House Association's "Be Our Special Guest," which mainly covers Down, Antrim, and Londonderry. The flood of tourists has been somewhat overwhelming.

We deeply appreciate the help from the Northern Ireland Tourist Board representatives in New York, Belfast, and Londonderry. We encourage you to avail yourself of their booking service. We found the staff in Belfast extremely courteous and welcoming. At their city or regional centers, maps, county guides, and event calendars are free. Also quality gifts, slide sets, audiotapes, and the like are available for a nominal price. For information in the U.S. call 1 (800) 326-0036 in New York; in Canada, 1 (416) 925-6368 in Toronto. There is an office in Dublin at 16 Nassau St., near the Blarney Woolen Mill shop. The Belfast office, which we found very useful, is at 59 North St. Telephone: 01232-246609. Park in the major car park nearby and walk there. People will be happy to direct you.

PRACTICAL MATTERS

We urge you to review our general advice on travel in the "Introduction to Ireland" at the beginning of the book. We won't repeat it here. These tips and advice apply as well to traveling in Northern Ireland. We have followed the same procedure and used the same standards in the North for the selection of B&Bs. Let us point out a few of the differences you can expect when you cross the border and give you some tips and advice to make your trip a great success.

Money and Changing Currency

Changing money can be a hassle, but it needn't be if you obtain American Express traveler's checks made out in pounds sterling. Most American Automobile Association offices have these for members free of charge at a reasonable exchange rate. By doing this you avoid running to a bank to exchange dollar traveler's checks and finding them closed. Our advice if you are going to tour both the South and the North, use both dollar traveler's checks in the South and sterling checks in the North. You won't be able to buy traveler's checks in Irish pounds (or punts) in the U.S.

Rental Cars

Some car rental companies do not allow you to take their car from the Republic of Ireland across the border. Check this out with your travel agent or your car rental company. Again remember MasterCard only provides you with collision insurance for 15 days overseas if you waive the insurance offered by the rental company. VISA Gold covers you for 30 days, a definite advantage if you are contemplating longer trips. Also as in the South, you drive on the opposite side of the road than you do in the U.S. Don't worry; it is easy and you will catch onto it in one day. We also find that automatic shifting is very helpful in reducing driving fatigue and in increasing ease of driving.

Booking Ahead

It is advisable to call ahead to book your next B&B stay. Most hosts will have recommendations for other B&Bs and might even call ahead for you. You can purchase a CALLCARD (or Phonecard) as in the South. These are not interchangeable with those in the Republic of Ireland. You have to buy a Northern one at the post office or some convenience stores. The rooms are priced per person unless otherwise noted. A single person will usually pay a higher rate. Currently many B&Bs are fully booked in the peak season. In June 1995, we couldn't find one room in Belfast within a reasonable price range. Northern Ireland has become a very popular tourist destination, so getting rooms in the better B&Bs like the ones in this book can be very difficult. That's why we urge you to make reservations ahead if you can. The codes to use are 011-44: drop the 0 from the 028 you'll find at the beginning of their numbers, then dial the rest of the number.

Rooms

Almost all of the other routines in B&Bs in Northern Ireland are the same as in the Republic of Ireland. You will see the abbreviation H&C in some listings. It means that there is a vanity or sink with a mirror in the room with hot and cold water. This allows you to wash up and brush your teeth without going to a shared bath. We bring light bathrobes and slippers for the shared bath when we occupy a standard room. These accommodations are generally cheaper than the rooms with a private bath. Frank likes the bigger mirror and sink in the shared bath when shaving, plus some shared baths have much larger showers or tub/showers than the baths en suite. We found the standards of both town and country homes and farm B&Bs in Northern Ireland to be excellent. We can't wait to go back to stay at some we could only visit for our usual interview and inspection. The rates are about the same, varying with the exchange rate of the English pound sterling instead of the Euro.

County Antrim

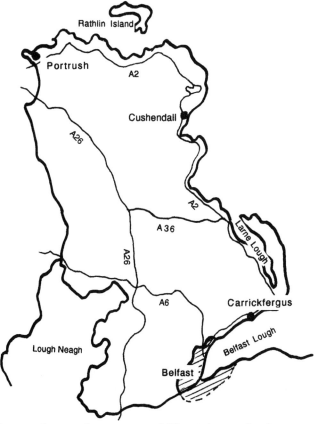

Antrim, on the northeast coast of Ulster, has majestic mountains that sweep down across grassy, green farm fields to the sea's edge, where rugged cliffs, white sandy beaches, and picturesque fishing villages form the boundary to the salty sea. The patchwork-quilt pattern of many shades of green and the man-made rock walls and farm fields complements the rest of the natural beauty and rivals those great vistas we have seen in the southwest of the Republic of Ireland and those in Cape Breton, Nova Scotia, or Hawaii. There are nine scenic glens to explore. Ulster's coastal outline on a map looks like a mirror image of the coast of Scotland—a mere 15 miles away. It is here you will also find many of Scottish ancestry; these are descendants of the Scots who migrated to Northern Ireland in hopes of finding a better life.

You can start at either end of the Antrim coast road and motor east from Portstewart or northwest from the Norman town of Carrickfergus and follow the rugged coast, up and down the high mountains and then down to the water's edge with a nice swimming beach at Cushendall. The beaches are safe, clean, and uncrowded—ideal for a day at the seaside. Many towns have seaside paths for hiking. The small ports will provide fishing trips and day cruises. Rathlin Island is a bird sanctuary that draws birders from all over the world to see the Razorbill colonies and other rare species. You can book a boat trip to Rathlin Island at Ballycastle and even stay at the island's sole B&B, the Rathlin Guest House. Horseback riding, golf, forest parks and farm museums, and many other recreational activities are available. In addition to the unique experience of exploring castles and ancient tombs and churches, we particularly enjoyed the 12th-century castle at Carrickfergus on the Belfast Lough, where full-sized mannequins dressed in armour or period garb adorn the walls and rooms and give more dimension to the visit. You can also see the Slemish Mountain at Broughshane, where St. Patrick is reputed to have herded swine as a slave after he was captured and brought to Ireland from England in the fifth century.

Legends abound in Irish history. Antrim has the Giant's Causeway with its story of the giant Finn MacCool and his walk to Scotland on the unusual rock formation that continues under the sea and rises out of the sea in Scotland. Another fun visit is a walk on the Carrick-a Rede Rope Bridge, high above the beach and ocean below, located 5 miles northwest of Ballycastle. There is Waterworld for the kids at Portrush and for us older folks, in the village of Bushmills, the Old Bushmill Distillery to liven your spirits. As you can see, there is much to do and see in Antrim.

Culbidagh House
Roisin and Charlie Hamill
115 Red Bay Road
Cushendall, County Antrim BT44 0SH
Telephone: 028-21771312
Bedrooms: 2 with private baths, 1 additional shower
Rates: £18-20; Discount for children under 12. Vouchers are accepted. **Credit cards:** None. **Open:** April 1 to November. **Children:** All ages. **Pets:** Outside only. **Smoking:** No. **Provisions for handicapped:** Yes, but must be able to do 6 steps. **Directions:** Take the coast road (A8) to Cushendall. As you come into town, look for the Culbidagh House sign on the left, just after the park on the right. Turn left and you will see Red Bay Boats, Ltd., on your right. Follow this street up to the top and turn left on Kilnadore Road. Go about a ½ mile; the street turns sharply right up the hill and becomes Red Bay Road. The Hamills' home is on your right, about a ½ mile farther.

This home has one of the most spectacular views in all of Northern Ireland. It is snuggled high on the hillside and overlooks sweeping green fields dotted with cows and grazing sheep, the town, and the Irish Sea far below. You can see the mountains of Scotland off in the northeast. Rooms have been redecorated in soft colors. One large room offers 2 double beds; another is at the front with table and chairs and a spectacular view. Charming Roisin and Charles work together to prepare your breakfast at a table in front of the bay windows with the panoramic view. They offer a delicious Irish Breakfast with choices of eggs, ham, sausage, fresh fruit, cereal, juice, and coffee or tea. Although there are golf, fishing, boating, and other watersports at the beach and park, we chose to hike along the Cliff Walk to the left of the beach and do some photography. The swimming was tempting as Ireland was experiencing a heat wave when we were there. Fran got up early one morning and attempted to scale the green-covered mountaintop off to one side of the property. She made it through several sheep pastures and above until even the house looked small in the distance below. The photos she took of fields, mist, and the sea below are prize winners. The evening's entertainment is watching the sunset and the mountains change color to red and rosy pink. It stays light until almost 10:30 P.M. during the summer because the North Pole is tilted toward the sun; but the temperature stays in the balmy, high 70s or 80s.

Maddybenny Farm House (and Riding Centre)
Rosemary White
Off Loguestown Road
Portrush, Coleraine
County Antrim BT52 2PT
Telephone: 02870-823394
Fax: 02870-822177
E-mail: accomodation@maddybenny22freeserve.co.uk
Bedrooms: 4, all with private baths, 6 self-catering cottages (4-star rated by NITB)
Rates: £25-30 p.p. bed and breakfast. Vouchers not accepted. 33 percent discount for children; write to Rosemary for details on cottage rentals. **Credit cards:** VISA and MasterCard. **Open:** January to November. **Children:** All ages. **Pets:** No. **Smoking:** Yes, except in dining room. **Provisions for handicapped:** None. **Directions:** Coming off A29 from Portrush, follow sign at Magherabuoy Hotel crossroads. From Coleraine north, follow signs to Riding Centre on A29 at Magherabuoy Road and Loguestown Road roundabout. Follow signs to Riding Centre and B&B Maddybenny.

This award-winning home has been recommended to us by many friends in Ireland. It is a Plantation Period farmhouse built before 1650 by the Earl of Antrim and completely renovated and furnished in fine family antiques. Horseback riding is available. The breakfasts have won the All Ireland Galtee Best Farmhouse Breakfast Award in 1989, 1992, and 1994. Before you turn in, Rosemary White asks that you read the menu and write down your order before you leave for the evening This will be your ticket to a gourmet and delicious breakfast by the Cordon Bleu cook. For example, the porridge can be taken with Drambuie, honey and cream. From there, you select 12 main dishes, including berries in season and muesli, several Fries, waffles, trout, and kippers. Bedrooms are large and all en suite, with color television, each capable of sleeping 4 people. Other amenities include: hospitality trays in rooms, refrigerator use in the hall for keeping your drinks and picnic things, pay phone in the hall, iron and ironing boards, and hair dryers and hot brushes. You also have full use of the cross-country and riding facilities and game room with snooker table. Mrs. White can direct you to local gourmet restaurants, Giant's causeway, seven golf courses, fishing, beaches and other tourist sites.

ALSO RECOMMENDED

Cushendall, *Cullentra House,* Olive McAuley. 16 Cloughs Road, BT 44 0SP. Telephone and Fax: 028-2177-1762. Ulster Tourist Development Association award winner. Nestled amidst breathtaking scenery of the Antrim Coast and Glens.

County Down

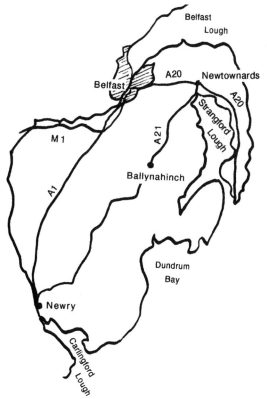

County Down borders on the Republic of Ireland, where people get their first glimpse of the North coming from Dublin and eastern areas. It presents wonderful first views of rolling green hills, wooden fences and wide roads. Newry, the first pretty town you'll visit, has an excellent little tourist bureau right in the Town Hall at the bridge in the town's center. Here you can also visit the Newry Arts Centre and Museum. At the head of Carlingford Lough, Newry is mostly a farm town, and you'll see the grazing sheep and cows very soon after you leave the town center. To the southeast, the stately purple Mourne Mountains can be seen for miles.

If you head for the seaside, you'll take the A2, or the coast road, to lovely Kilkeel, where you can enjoy the beaches, watch fishing boats, and visit Green's Castle. Going north to Newcastle, you'll pass Donard Cave and Maggie's Leap. In the port of Newcastle, walk the promenade or go swimming, boating, or ponytrekking along the beach. You can camp at Tollymore Forest Park, where there is a great wildlife reserve.

Downpatrick is a fascinating area, with the cathedral overlooking the Quoile River, and the stone grave of Saint Patrick. This is where Saint Patrick lived out his last days in A.D. 46. You may want to visit the ruins of Saint Tassach's Church near Saul, where he took his last Holy Communion. Cross over to Portaferry and the peninsula of beauty along Strangford Lough. Greyabbey has not only the famed Grey Abbey, but it is an "antique heaven." Farther north, visit the charming Mount Stewart House and acres of gardens on the way to Newtownards. Strangford Lough, which opens out to the sea, is so large it would be called a bay in America. These towns along the water's edge have gorgeous beaches and views.

From Newtownards you're only a half-hour from Belfast, if you drive during the midday. Here you'll find an astonishing city with many Victorian buildings that hearken back to the days of linen-making and shipbuilding. There are some boarded-up windows, but you'd hardly notice that fighting and guns used to be the order of the day. They've done some lavish reconstruction of the downtown area with many streets closed off to all traffic but shopping buses. Well-known storefronts of classy design line these streets, and it's safe to walk anywhere since peace has been established. Visit the huge, glittering multistoried shopping mall called Castlecourt Centre that is off Royal Avenue. The wonderful Northern Irish Tourist Bureau, situated in the town center at 59 North St., will give you help in all directions. Sheila Cameron and Maureen Campbell were especially tireless and very generous with their attention to us. Their phone number is 01232 or 0-800-317153 (credit cards only).

Not far away at the end of High Street is the famed Albert Memorial Clock Tower and the Anglican St. Anne's Cathedral. We enjoyed a delicious and reasonable lunch at the handsome Deer's Head Pub across from the Tourist Board. Other good pubs are White's Tavern, built in 1630, and the famous Victorian Crown Liquor Saloon at 46 Great Victoria St. One B&B owner sent us for an excellent Italian meal to Gigolo's Restaurant at 23 Donegal Pass Rd. Not only does the charming owner come out of the kitchen to explain his splendid recipes, but at night he'll serenade you with Italian arias. Visit the rococo Grand Opera House on Great Victoria Street with all of its gold trim. Here they hold plays, musical operas, and a children's theater. The Lyric Theater also has plays and music. In November, the Belfast Arts Festival at Queen's University has hundreds of cultural events. Don't pass up a tour of the grand old City Hall with its lovely marble inside. Of course, you'll want to see the beautiful Botanic Gardens.

If you were to continue north on the A24 from Downpatrick, you'd reach the historic town of Ballynahinch with its wide streets. It was the scene of a battle in 1798, where 7,000 United Irishmen died trying to take the city. Go southwest from this town to see Northern Ireland's best known Neolithic dolmen, the Legananny, with its large delicately balanced stones.

Edenvale House
Diane and Gordon Whyte
130 Portaferry Road
Newtownards, County Down BT22 2AH
Telephone: 02891-814881
Fax: 02891-826192
E-mail: edenvalehouse@hotmail.com
Bedrooms: 3 with private baths
Rates: £27.50-35. Discounts for children. Vouchers not accepted.
Credit cards: VISA and MasterCard. **Open:** January 2 to December 23.
Children: All ages. **Pets:** Yes. **Smoking:** Restricted to sunroom. **Provisions for handicapped:** Only if they can manage stairs. **Directions:** It is on the east side of Strangford Lough, about 2 miles south of the town of Newtonards and the Flying Club on the Belfast-Portaferry Road (A20). Before the stone pillar entrance, there is a large Butterlump Rock on the beach to your right and a row of cottages on your left. The small Edenvale House sign at the entrance on the left is easy to miss. It is before Mount Stewart Garden. *A note of caution:* This is a dangerous entrance when leaving; enter the road slowly.

This elegant 1780 Georgian house, furnished with antiques, fresh flowers, and open log fires, is a part of a seven-acre farm, and Diane and Gordon Whyte keep six horses but not for riding. Stables are available FREE for horses or dogs. Mrs. Whyte gave us a friendly full Irish welcome with a tea and delicious strawberry tarts on the patio outside the sunroom. From here we had a perfect view across the lough to the Mourne Mountains. Their dogs will greet you as well. The three rooms in this beautifully renovated home are all carpeted and feature large, tastefully decorated baths. Antiques grace all of the rooms. One has a large, canopied, king-sized bed with soft green and pink decor; another is pale blue and yellow. A new room is on the second floor with a lake view, fourposter bed, and dressing room. The living room is roomy and the country kitchen with hanging herbs is sunny and inviting. This B&B looks like something out of *House Beautiful* or *Home and Garden* magazines. Their breakfast of hot homemade breads, fried potato bread, and hot fruit complete with cream, along with the traditional Irish breakfast, will not be forgotten. Places to visit in the area are the world-famous Mount Stewart Garden and Estate, antique shops in Greyabbey, and Castle Espie Wildlife Centre. For the sports minded, there is golf, sailing, wind surfing, riding, and bird watching.

ALSO RECOMMENDED

Kilkeel, *Kilmorey Arms Hotel,* Owner: Peter Houston, 41-43 Greencastle Street. Telephone: 028-4176-2220. Bedrooms: 26, all en suite. Discount for seniors. Evening meal available. Delightful small inn with homey atmosphere. Accepts credit cards. Nice cocktail lounge and public bar, worthy of a pint or two if passing through Kilkeel, or if you're thirsty from a walk in the Mournes.

COUNTY FERMANAGH

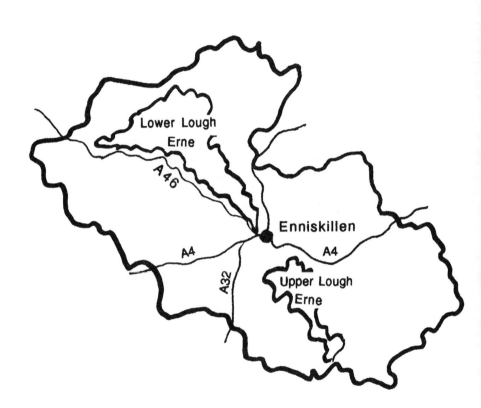

County Fermanagh

County Fermanagh is a region of rolling hills and farms, but Lough Erne and its upper and lower loughs with its enchanting and historic islands dominate the region. And where the lake and inland waterway appear pinched off in the middle stands the ancient town of Enniskillen. Plan to spend some time here and revel in the beauty of the lakes and mystical and enchanting quality of the ancient tales. Many a struggle for control of this strategic town was fought here. In those medieval times when there was peace, you can almost imagine the lords and ladies gathering at Enniskillen Castle for dinner and poetry reading after the men returned from the hunt.

This restored castle keep and barracks is a must for its display of past life in this region, its natural history, regimental museum, and a room dedicated to the life and work of a famous porcelain artist from Enniskillen. Also, while at the castle, be sure to view the excellent videos on the second floor of the museum that tell the story of Enniskillen past and present and the romantic stories of the Maguires who fought for and against the British. The Buttermarket is now a craft center where you can buy lace, knitwear, and Belleek china. To see this distinctive porcelain being made, go to Belleek Village, 25 miles away where the Erne rushes to meet the Atlantic.

South of Enniskillen on the A4 is Castle Coole, a splendid neoclassical mansion set on the shore of Lough Coole and surrounded by a parkland. Also the 18th-century, three-story manor home, Florence Court, about 8 miles southwest of Enniskillen via the A4 and A32, is another place you must visit. For those interested in caves and cool places, the Marble Arch Caves near Florence Court, which are reported to be one of the most awesome sights in Europe, provide you with a boat ride and all the spectacles associated with large underground cave systems. Call ahead for an update on current hours of operation (Telephone: 01365-348855). For horse and equestrian fans there is the Ulster Equestrian Centre at Necarne, Irvinestown (Telephone: 013656-21919).

Lackaboy Farm
Mrs. Derrick Noble
Tempo Road
Enniskillen, County Fermanagh BT74 4RH
Telephone: 02866-322488
Fax: 02866-320440
Bedrooms: 6 with private baths
Rates: £25-40 p.p.; 50 percent discount for children. Vouchers accepted. £12 dinner (4 courses). **Credit cards:** VISA, Access, and MasterCard. **Open:** All year, except Christmas. **Children:** All ages; babysitting available. **Pets:** No. **Smoking:** No **Provisions for handicapped:** None **Directions:** Take the B80 out of Enniskillen. Go about 1 mile. You'll see the guesthouse sign. Turn left and follow Tempo Road for a few hundred yards. Past a paddock and opposite the Fermanagh Agricultural Centre, you will see Lackaboy Farm on the left. It has a low, whitewalled entrance that leads to the white, two-storied farmhouse.

Lackaboy Farm guesthouse is part of a dairy farm with 45 Fresian cows. Using a century-old foundation, the Nobles rebuilt the house in keeping with the character of the original home. It is notable for its Amishlike simplicity, neatness, and charm. The seven rooms are all large and attractively redecorated, with televisions and new bathrooms. All have flowered duvets and views of the farm and surrounding hills. All have H&C. For breakfast Mrs. Noble has a trolley of cereals, fruit, and cheese along with her traditional Irish breakfast and her brewed coffee. She offers a scrumptious four-course dinner if you book ahead. At the Fermanagh Agricultural Centre across the street, livestock auctions and horse shows are held. This farm is just outside historic Enniskillen, which serves as a connecting channel for the upper and lower parts of Lough Erne. Golf courses are nearby. As we walked along side the lough in the castle park one evening after having a delicious meal at Mulligan's (33-35 Darling St.), we saw holiday seekers cruising in their rented yachts and young people practicing in their racing shells for an upcoming tournament. Ducks were swimming among the bullrushes. This was a beautiful scene that begged to be painted. This farm was recommended to us as a special place by many northern Irish who like to come here and relax for a week at a time. Scenic drives, fishing, golf, the theatre and leisure centre, and ten-pin bowling are all nearby.

COUNTY LONDONDERRY

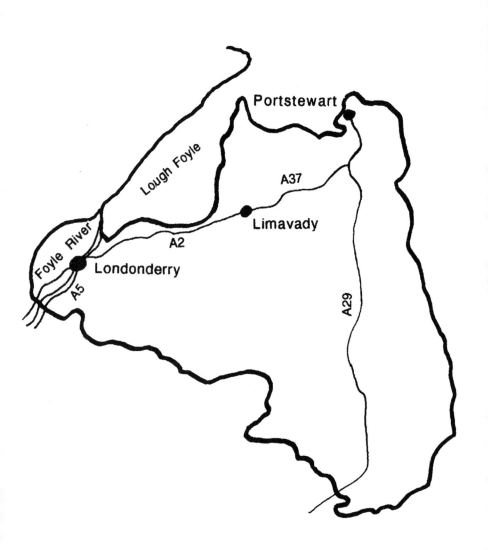

County Londonderry

St. Columb came out of Donegal 1,400 years ago and founded his first monastery in the oak grove (Doire in Gaelic), a gift from his cousin, Prince of Ailech. It was a holy place. The saint said that "the angels of God sang in the glades of Derry and every leaf held its angel."

Londonderry is the second largest city in Northern Ireland and borders on Donegal. This beautiful city with its massive medieval walls and four gates perched on the banks of Lough Foyle presents a wonderful opportunity for a walking tour of the 1633 Gothic cathedral of St. Columb, the ornate Victorian Guildhall, and the many shops and pubs. We enjoyed our pub grub pints at J & T McGinleys (24 Foyle Street) after we toured the city. It is an excellent pub with character and history, formerly owned by a tea merchant. We did not see or hear of any troubles in Derry while we were in Northern Ireland, so one should not be fearful of fully enjoying the sights and sounds of this historic and scenic city.

The countryside of Derry spreads over a flat plain from the city to Limavady and Coleraine. If you take the A2 north on the west side of Limavady you will be able to complete a scenic loop of the Roe Valley and over the mountain top drive of Mt. Bineveneagh beginning on the north coast turning south at Downhill, or continue on the coastal A2 to Coleraine, past the Mussenden Temple built by an eccentric Bishop of Derry as testimony of his affection for Mrs. Musssenden. The main road from Coleraine to Limavady on the A37 is equally breathtaking in its panoramic view of the valley to the west. Limavady is where Jane Ross penned the tune of the famous "Londonderry Air" ('Danny Boy'), which she heard a passing fiddler play. Another attraction is the Roe Valley Country Park 2 miles south of Limavady via the B192. A restored old linen mill and hydroelectric station built in 1896 are on the grounds with a museum. Activities at the park include canoeing, fishing, picnicking, and rock climbing. The most northeastern town in Londonderry is Portstewart, which is astride the Magilligan Strand. The longest beach in Ireland, the Magilligan Strand is formed where the Bann River empties into the Atlantic.

Ballyhenry House
Rosemary Kane
172 Seacoast Road
Limavady, County Londonderry BT49 9EF
Telephone: 028-77722657
Bedrooms: 3, 1 with private, 2 with shared baths
Rates: £20 p.p.; Shared £18-20; Single £22-25; 33 percent discount for children. Vouchers accepted. Dinner offered at £12.50. **Credit cards:** None. **Open:** All year. **Children:** All ages. **Pets:** Outside. **Smoking:** No. **Provisions for handicapped:** Partial. **Directions:** Take the A2 from Coleraine to Limavady. As you leave Limavady headed toward Londonderry Town, you will cross the Roe River Bridge. At the end of the bridge, at the light, turn right or north onto the B69. After 3.3 miles toward Downhill, you will see the colorful sign for the farm on the left. From Derry, turn left at the light at the end of the Roe River Bridge. The directions remain the same as above.

Ballyhenry House is a lovely, airy 1890 farmhouse , built by the Kane family. It has a large, catchy, bright-colored sign featuring a farmer with a scythe. The Kane family raises seed wheat and barley and has more than 100 sheep and fifty cattle on this 1901 farm. The four bedrooms are spacious and sunny and have great pastoral views. One of the rooms was bright yellow and the one where we stayed had soothing lavender-and-blue wallpaper with matching bedspreads and wall-to-wall rugs. One room has original floors and is done in denim blue and yellow. All have sinks in the rooms and shared baths. One new large family room has a balcony. Rosemary Kane serves an Irish breakfast with choice of fresh fruit in season, porridge, yogurt, cereal, and teas and coffee. The house sits on a flat plain in clear veiw of the steep Binevenagh Mountain. Mrs. Kane sent us on a short car ride up the 384-meter mountain, which we took in late evening after dinner, for a grand view of the mountains of Donegal, Lough Foyle to the west, and the sea to the north. We spent a long time up there watching some young men haying in the dimming light of sunset around 10:30 P.M. An enchanting and romantic sight! It's a fascinating area when you realize there is nothing else between you and the North Pole but the Hebrides and a few scattered islands. There is also golf, horse-riding, fishing, a Roe Valley Country Park for picnicking, bird watching, walks, ponytrekking, and hang-gliding in the area. It is only 5-7 miles from the beach. A bird sanctuary and a museum, as well as the bustling town of Limavady, are nearby. Also, the many attractions of the large city of Londonderry are not far away. The Giant's Causeway is only ³/₄ of an hour away by car.

Elagh Hall
Elizabeth Buchanan
Buncrana Road
Londonderry Town, County Londonderry BT48 8LU
Telephone: 028-71263116
E-mail: lizelagh@yahoo.com
Bedrooms: 3; 2 with private baths, 1 with shared
Rates: £20 p.p. private bath; £18 p.p. shared bath; 50 percent discount
for children. Vouchers accepted. **Credit cards:** None. **Open:** From
April to September. **Children:** All ages. **Pets:** No. **Smoking:** No. **Provisions for handicapped:** None. **Directions:** From Londonderry, take
Buncrana Road (A2) about 2 miles, then turn right at Elagh Road
(first right after BP Station).

This 1795 farmhouse is set on 100 acres of rich farmland where the
owners raise mostly sheep and cattle. This was the manse for the Burt
Presbyterian Church just across the border in Donegal. It was purchased by John Buchanan's father in 1948 and it has been in the family ever since. The house is handsomely decorated with antique
furniture and all of the rooms have views of either Grianan Castle or
the Donegal Hills. Elizabeth offers a full Irish breakfast, and her specialties are homemade jams (raspberry, strawberry, and black-currant from berries grown in her own garden). The house has an
Old-World atmosphere, like a step back in time. You wake up in the
morning to lovely fresh air, singing birds, and sheep bleating in meadows below. Templemore Sports Complex is 1 mile away; there are 2
golf courses; fishing, horseback riding, beautiful sandy beaches, are
nearby. The Buchanans highly recommend Harry's restauraunt,
which is not far from Elagh Hall.

County Tyrone

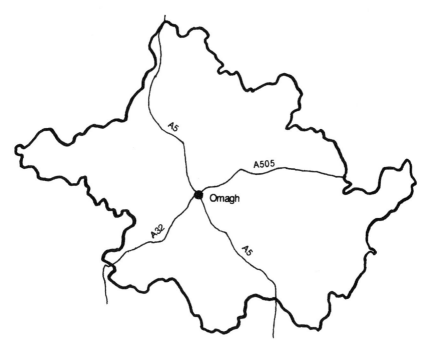

When we first drove up to County Tyrone from Monaghan, we were struck with the pretty green rolling hills and neat farmlands with fertile valleys. Farther north there are the majestic Sperrin Mountains, which are excellent for walks through fields with grazing sheep, yellowed in the mild winter by whin or gorse (juniper). Dyeing boiled eggs in whin to color them yellow is an Easter custom.

At Strabane you can see some special Tyrone countryside if you drive southeast on the B47 through the Sperrin Mountains to Draperstown, south on the B162 to Cookstown, and then west to Omagh on the A505—stop at a pub or two along the way to quench your thirst. Farther north from Omagh is Gortin with the Sperrin Heritage Center, where there are gold-mining and natural history exhibits, a craft shop, and a cafe. One of our favorite stops (where you will want to spend at least a half-day) is the Ulster-American Folk Park. Its main theme is the history of the eighteenth- and nineteenth-century Ulster emigration to North America. Original homes, one from the ancestors of the Mellon family (who endowed the park), are arranged in tree-lined paths, and each one tells in chronological order the story of the Ulster Irish in America, the covered wagons, the sod prairie houses—even a large ship that you can board to see the appalling conditions endured by the emigrants en route to America. It is very creative and educational as well as great fun. A café is there at the entrance for teas and light meals.

Neolithic sites include the Beaghmore stone circles at Cookstown, which were uncovered only 40 years ago, and the chambered cairn of Knockmany at the top of a steep wooded hill north of Clogher. At Ardboe there is an 18-foot Celtic cross. Another Celtic feature is the 14th-century Gaelic stronghold in West Tryone: Harry Avery's Castle. The ancestral home of Woodrow Wilson is at Strabane and his farm is still kept open by the Wilsons, who will show callers around the house. We almost lost count of the number of American presidents with Ulster roots or ancestors. Antrim has five alone!

Greenmount Lodge Country House
Louie Reid
58 Greenmount Road
Gortaclare
Omagh, County Tyrone BT79 0YE
Telephone: 028-82841325
Fax: 028-82840019
E-mail: greenmountlodge@lineone.net
Bedrooms: 8, all en suite
Rates: £20 p.p.; Single £25; £12.50 and up for dinner; 50 percent discount for children. **Credit cards:** Yes. **Open:** January to December. **Children:** All ages. **Pets:** No. **Smoking:** No. **Provisions for handicapped:** Yes, the best accommodations in the area (NITB Category 1 classification). **Directions:** Off of the A5 (or Omagh to Ballygawley Road), about 8 miles south of Omagh town or 7 miles from Ballygawly, turn right after the Carrick Keel/Pub toward Beagh. The sign for Greenmount is on the left after the four-way intersection. The house is one mile farther on the left.

This lovely Grade-A farm bed and breakfast, really a historical country estate, is set in the tranquility of 150 acres of beautiful scenery. West Tyrone is a surprising mixture of bleak, brownish boglands with whaleback hills that are separated by fertile valleys and rich pastures. Award-winning Greenmount Lodge has luxury accommodations that draw rave reviews from many guests from different countries. One guest wrote, "The host and hostess make us feel as though we are their sole guests." Their guest book sings out "Excellent" in many languages. The guest rooms are fashionably decorated and the beds are comfortable. Bathtubs have been added to some rooms. There is a guest laundry room. The full Irish breakfast is begun with a buffet table of "starters" of various cereals, oats, fresh fruits, juices, and yogurts. Fish and vegetarian dishes are also available on request. The Reids can accommodate most dietary requirements. The "sweet table" on weekends is reputed to be the best in Ireland. Having hosted guests for 25 years, the Reids will provide you with warm hospitality, good food, and a relaxing atmosphere. As they are on the northwest passage, this will make an ideal "base camp" for exploring the many parks, castles, museums, and natural and historical features of the region. They give 10 percent off cash payments and a good discount for booking direct with credit cards. Play tennis on their new court, golf, fish, or do game shooting nearby. Great walks near lakes and visit the Visitor American Folk Park. We enjoyed it.

Self-Catering

This new section introduces travelers to the world of self-catering lodgings, which, as the name implies, means we (the innkeepers) supply the utensils, you do the cooking, we supply the bedding, you make the beds and keep house. The operators of most self-catering accommodations will show you the property, show you how to operate the equipment and appliances, take readings on the gas and/or oil for heating and cooking, and orient you to the neighborhood service, and then bid you adieu until you leave. A deposit is taken at the booking or reservation, and the agent or owner will meet you at the door or guide you to the place. Be sure they leave their home phone number so you can ask them questions as they arise.

Our experience is that this is a great, cost-effective alternative for traveling families. You can save money over staying in a bed and breakfast, guesthouse, or hotel, and it gives you freedom and flexibility over when you do things. You are not tied down with someone else's schedule. You also get to experience the Ireland like a native, shopping in grocery stores, going to dry cleaning, getting a haircut, and the like. For kids, they have the outlet of their own home, the privacy of their own bedroom, and the fun of walking to neighborhood shops.

This section will identify recommended places, some of which the authors or friends have stayed at. We have selected accommodations in places where you might want to stay for at least a week, at the top tourist spots. In selecting a place, the demeanor of the host is important and you will have to judge what kind of person you are dealing with. But you usually can tell after a few phone calls how hospitable they are. This is an important consideration in booking self-catering. Weekly rates are quoted: the low rate is off season, the high rate is peak season—July and August. The number of bedrooms and how many they sleep might not agree since a couch or cot might be counted. Utilities are extra. In the off season, the rate can usually be negotiated. The location of accommodation is listed first in bold, and the address (which will be somewhere else) of owner and agent is given. The first telephone number will be the owners, the second may be an association number or booking service.

REPUBLIC OF IRELAND

Dublin City and County

Clontarf, Mrs. Nan and Patrick Lowe, 207 Sutton Place, Sutton, Dublin 13. Telephone/Fax: 01-8324209, 800-866-866-88. Bedrooms: 2-bedroom. Superbly situated modern townhouse, 3-star, adjacent to Clontarf Castle. Sleeps 4. €470 June-October. Rest of year on request. We recommend this townhouse, as it is in a lovely and upscale part of suburban Dublin, close to public transport and good restaurants. You can walk to Drawbridge Pub in Castle for lunch.

Clontarf, Mrs. Maeve and James McKenna, 6 Seacourt, Seafield Road East, Clontarf, Dublin 3. Telephone: 01-8330185. Fax: (066) 9792116. Same 3 star townhouse complex as above, only larger, with 3 bedrooms. Sleeps 6. €457-571.

Rathcoole, Mrs. Brid Fitzpatrick, Shamrock Lodge, Castlewarden, Straffen, County Kildare. Telephone: 01-4588327. Fax: 01-4580475. 4 bedrooms, 3-star detached house. Sleeps 6. Suburb south of Dublin City Center. Very nice owner, good access to Wicklow and Kildare. €350-470

Templeogue, David Brophy, 12 Nutley Lane, Dublin 4. Telephone: 01-269-1309. Fax: 066-9792116. Bedrooms: 3. Sleeps 6. Modern semidetached house. South Dublin suburb. €280-440.

Southeast

Ballon, Mary Jordan, Milltown, Kilbride, Ballon, County Carlow. Farmhouse on tillage farm near owner's residence. Nature's paradise. Telephone and fax: 0503-59136. Tel: 0503-59939. Bedrooms: 3. Sleeps 6. €254-380.

Inistioge, Margaret Dunne, St. Columb's Presbytery, Kilmacshane, Inistioge, County Kilkenny. Telephone and fax: 056-58550, 800-866-866-88. E-mail: stcolumb@gofree.indigo.ie. 2 bedrooms. Sleeps 5. Eighteenth-century coach house. 4 star. Beautiful setting in Nore River Valley. €247-399

Kilkenny, Joan and Kevin Mahon, The Gables, Archersgrove, Kilkenny, County Kilkenny. Telephone: 056-61869. Fax: 056-51788. Winner of Agritourism Award. Restored eighteenth-century house on deer farm. 3 bedrooms. Sleeps 5. 3 star. €275-375. Off-season rates by request.

Southwest

Bantry, Mary Coakley, Snave, Bantry, County Cork. Telephone: 027-50902. Bedrooms: 4, 3 en suite. Sleeps 8. Bungalow in scenic location overlooking Bantry Bay. 5-minute walk to sea. 3 star. €190-571.

Kinsale, Clare O'Donovan, Laurel Wood House, Ballinhassig, County Cork. Telephone 021-4885103. Fax: 021-4885103. Bedrooms: 2. Sleeps 4. House within 5 minutes of picturesque Kinsale. €254-480.

Dingle, Teresa Devane, 20 Meadowlands, Oakpark, Tralee, County Kerry. Telephone: 066-7126169 (after 6 P.M.). Bedrooms: 4. Sleeps 8. 3 star. Two-story house overlooking Ventry Harbor and beach. €300-500. Rest of year by request.

Killarney, Helen Foran, Ard Na Griene, Tralee Road, Killarney County Kerry. Telephone: 064-31778/021-273251. Fax: 066-9792116. 4 bedrooms. Sleeps 8 comfortably. Detached modern house with garden. Fully furnished in all regards. Wonderfully accommodating owner. Just outside Killarney off Tralee Road in country setting. €253-571.

Shannon

Doolin, Breda Cullinan, Ballyvara, Doolin, County Clare. Telephone 065-7074349. Fax: 066-9792116. Bedrooms: 2. Sleeps 4. Traditional thatched cottage on Main Cliff of Moher Road. 1 km from Doolin. Renowned for its traditional music and seafood. 1 star. €190-380.

Lahinch, Sheila Kelleher, Ennistymon Road, Lahinch, County Clare. Telephone: 065-7081234 (work), 065-7081262 (home). Fax: 065-7081223. Bedrooms: 3. Sleeps 6. 4 star. Beautifully decorated house. All amenities, even BBQ. €255-575. Rest of year on request.

Ireland West—Galway

Clifden, Moira King, Boat Harbour, Errislannan, County Galway. Telephone: 095-21467. Bedrooms: 4, 1 en suite. Sleeps 8. Modern, large, 3-star bungalow, view of sea and lakes. €317.43-571.38.

Galway (Sea Road), George Clancy, Crescent Close, Sea Road, Galway, County Galway. Telephone: 091-587338. Fax: 091-537780. Bedrooms: 3. Sleeps 5. 3-star apartments. In Salthill, beach within walking distance, close to Galway city and amenities. €444-508.

Galway West—Mayo

Westport, Jacqueline and Frank Brady, Newtown House, Partry, Claremorris, County Mayo. Telephone: 092-43009/091-537777. Fax: 091-537780. Bedrooms: 3. Sleeps 5. New, modern, two-story, 3-star house.

Within walking distance of town. Close to beach, golf, and fishing. Many features. €320-440.

Northwest—Donegal

Donegal Town, Brian Espey, Summerhill, Donegal Town, County Donegal. Telephone: 073-21327. Bedrooms: 3. Sleeps 5. Semidetached house 4 km from Donegal Town. Magnificent views of Donegal Bay, islands, and mountains. Beach .5 mile. 2 star. €165-380.

NORTHERN IRELAND

(Rates in pound sterling)

Antrim

Cushendun, Anne Blaney, 114 Tromra Road, Cushendum, County Antrim. BT44 0ST. Telephone/Fax: 021667-61221. E-mail: mullarts@1dpt.demon.co.uk. 4 star. Located between Cushendall and Cushendun on Antrim Coast. Converted church into three award-winning apartments. Two sleeps 2, and one sleeps 5. £200-375

Portrush, Rosemary White, 18 Maddybenny Park, Portrush, County Antrim. BT52 2 PT. Telephone/Fax: 02870-823394. 6 mews cottages. Sleeps 6/8. Pretty equestrian center on the coast. 4 star. £250-450.

Down

Newcastle, D. Maginn, Tory Bush Cottages. 79 Tullyree Road, Bryansford, Newcastle, County Down. Telephone: 013967-24348. 8 traditional cottages. Sleeps 5. 3 star. Situated in middle Mourne Mountains, 4 miles from coastal resort of Newcastle. Many recreational features nearby. Beautiful vistas. £250-410.

Fermanagh

Enniskillen, C. McManus, Teemore, Derrylin, Count Fermanagh, BT92 9BL. Telephone/Fax: 013657-48493. 6 bungalows. Sleeps 3/6. On the Shannon-Erne canal link. 3 star. Day cruisers can be rented to explore the pleasures of the waterway and to explore neighboring villages. £200-360.

Index

LODGINGS
(County in parentheses)

NORTHERN IRELAND CITIES AND TOWNS

LODGINGS
(County in parentheses)

PLEASE HELP US
TO KEEP OUR STANDARDS HIGH

To help maintain the high reputation of *The Irish Bed &*
Breakfast Book, we ask for your comments about your stay. It will
help us if you return all comment forms in one envelope.

Name of Host _____

Address _____

It was (please circle one):
Absolutely Perfect, Excellent, Good, Adequate, Not Satisfactory.

Do you have any comments that could help your host, on such
things as breakfast, meals, beds, cleanliness, hospitality, or value
for money?

Complete this section. It will be detached before we send your
comments to the host.

YOUR NAME _____

YOUR ADDRESS _____

_____

Please mail this form to Pelican Publishing Co. Inc.
P.O. Box 3110, Gretna, LA 70054-3110, USA

FOLD HERE. FASTEN LIP ON FRONT WITH CLEAR TAPE.

PLEASE FASTEN SIDES WITH CLEAR TAPE.

PLEASE FASTEN SIDES WITH CLEAR TAPE.

CUT

FOLD HERE

RE: 5th edition, Irish B&B

PLACE
FIRST-CLASS
POSTAGE

IRISH B&B
Pelican Publishing Company
1000 Burmaster Street
P.O. Box 3110
Gretna, Louisiana 70054-3110

THIS IS DUBLIN POCKET GUIDE

By Myles Plunkett

This two-in-one guide and removable, waterproof, Tyvek city map are the perfect touring companions to the enigmatic capital of the Emerald Isle.

The birthplace of James Joyce, home of Trinity College and the *Book of Kells,* and location of the Guinness Brewery, Dublin truly has something to offer for everyone.

Directions for three classic walks are provided and include a tour of Dublin pubs. Excursions outside Dublin are detailed as well, as are places to stay, eat, shop, and be lively. And with the extremely handy removable city map, Dublin is literally at your fingertips . . . or in your pocket.

112 pp. 4³⁄₄ x 8¹⁄₄
56 color photos 3 b/w photos 1 illus.
5 color maps plus separate city map Index
ISBN: 1-56554-683-0 pb

TO ORDER ANY OF THESE BOOKS DIRECTLY FROM PELICAN, PLEASE CALL TOLL FREE

1-800-843-1724

THE SCOTTISH BED & BREAKFAST BOOK

By June Skinner Sawyers

A Glasgow native shares lodging secrets she has learned on her yearly return visits to her homeland.

From the opulent Sibbet House in Edinburgh to the romantic Old Smiddy in the Highlands, bed and breakfasts in Scotland offer premier lodgings for every taste and budget.

208 pp. 5½ x 8½
60 illus. 12 maps Index
ISBN: 1-56554-651-2 pb

THE MAVERICK GUIDE TO SCOTLAND

By June Skinner Sawyers

"*Maverick Guide to Scotland* offers lots of detail (including glossaries of regional speech and listings of local tourist information centers). The author . . . brings a wealth of knowledge to her subject . . . an especially wise purchase. Recommended for public libraries."

—*Library Journal*

608 pp. 5½ x 8½
19 maps 54 photos
Appendix Index
ISBN: 1-56554-227-4 pb

GOLFING IN IRELAND
The Most Complete Guide for Adventurous Golfers, 2nd Edition

By Rob Armstrong

Ireland is one of the most popular golf venues for Americans who are eager to sample famous links golf courses like Ballybunion and Lahinch.

In the first edition, author Rob Armstrong predicted the Irish golf boom. In his thoroughly revised second edition, he revisits old golf courses and profiles the best new ones, including County Cork's magnificent Old Head Golf Club, already regarded as one of the most exciting new courses in the world.

256 pp. 6 x 9
36 photos 28 scorecards
Appendixes Index
ISBN: 1-56554-726-8 pb

THE BOOK OF IRISH GOLF

By John Redmond

Discover all of the aspects of Irish golf, from the courses and competitors of its early days to the new courses and players who are emerging and adding to its legacy at home and abroad. The author takes the reader back to some of the greatest moments in Irish golf and presents statistics and records that have been set on Irish courses. Stunning photographs of the historic courses as well as many notable competitors are included.

176 pp. 8½ x 11
Color and b/w photos Index
ISBN: 1-56554-327-0 hc

THE AUSTRALIAN BED & BREAKFAST BOOK
13th Edition

Compiled by J. & J. Thomas

This thoroughly updated guide lists prices, facilities, addresses, illustrations of the various homes, and telephone numbers for making reservations, along with easy-to-follow directions. For ten years, this has been the premier guide to Australian B&Bs.

464 pp. 5½ x 8½
Illus. Maps Index 13th ed.
ISBN: 1-58980-030-3 pb